Ancient Peoples and Places

PERU

General Editor

DR GLYN DANIEL

DR GLYN DANIEL *Ancient Peoples and Places*

PERU

G. H. S. Bushnell
M.A., Ph.D.

71 PHOTOGRAPHS
11 LINE DRAWINGS
AND A MAP

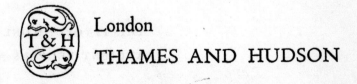

London
THAMES AND HUDSON

THIS IS VOLUME ONE IN THE SERIES
ANCIENT PEOPLES AND PLACES

CONTENTS

ILLUSTRATIONS

7

8

Preface

IN THE DECADE following the end of the Second World War there has been a considerable and growing interest in archaeology, particularly in prehistoric and protohistoric archaeology, which deals with the ancient peoples and places of the world. There are now in English many books introducing the aims and methods of archaeology, and describing the broad general conclusions of prehistory, but there is a great need for small books which take a limited area or a single people and set forth the current state of knowledge about it in a way attractive to the non-specialist archaeologist as well as the ordinary interested reader. It is to fill this gap that we have designed this series: in each book we intend, with the aid of the written word and numerous illustrations, to bring to life a specific people or place in the ancient world.

This book on Peru, by Dr. Geoffrey Bushnell, the Curator of the Cambridge University Musuem of Archaeology and Ethnology, is the first volume in the series. It will be followed shortly by *The Scythians,* by Tamara Talbot Rice, which will contain much material hitherto unpublished in English. Books in active preparation range over the ancient countries and nations of the world; from the Celts and Phoenicians and the Vikings to Sicily, Wales and Wessex. We hope also to include sometimes books dealing with quite small areas of exceptional interest such as the great Boyne cemetery in Ireland which contains New Grange and Dowth, or the north Wessex area which has such important and remarkable monuments as Windmill Hill, Silbury Hill and Avebury.

It is not intended that these volumes should as a series comprehend all the ancient past in time and space—that would surely be impossible. Rather we hope that they should deal with peoples and places of general interest when experts are available ready and willing to embark on the difficult and often thankless task of being popular without being pompous or patronizing. Dr. Bushnell sounds the right note. He brings to his subject a wealth of learning and presents it in a clear and palatable form. In this way we hope to achieve our aim—to bring the ancient peoples and places of the world—or at least some of them—within the comprehension of everyone.

GLYN DANIEL

Foreword

OUR KNOWLEDGE of Ancient Peru has increased very rapidly in recent years, and most of this new information is set out in papers and handbooks published by universities, museums and scientific institutions in the United States, or privately circulated in Peru. Most of these publications are not available in this country, except in a few specialized libraries, and not all of them are even to be found there. P. A. Means published a general work called *Ancient Civilizations of the Andes* in the United States in 1931, but the latest book to be published in Great Britain was T. A. Joyce's admirable *South American Archaeology*, which appeared in 1912. Both contain much that is worth reading, but in the nature of things they are very much out of date. There is a most excellent general account of Peruvian archaeology in *Andean Culture History* by Bennett See *Bibliography* and Bird, to which I am greatly indebted, but it was published just before the first results of radiocarbon dating became avail, able. Being a museum handbook, it has not a wide circulation, even in the United States. To all of these sources, to the study of museum collections in Great Britain, France and the United States, and to visits to Peru in 1938 and 1951, I owe the in, formation presented in this book.

Pottery and other objects from the middle and later parts of the archaeological succession are abundant in museums in Great Britain and elsewhere, and photographs for illustration are easily obtained, but material from the early cultures, which were unknown until a few years ago, is very rare outside Peru. For this reason, I am particularly grateful to my friend Señor Rafael Larco Hoyle, of Lima and the Hacienda Chiclin, near Trujillo, for the magnificent photographs of Cupisnique, Salinar, Virú (Gallinazo) and other pottery, which add distinction to our series of plates. The subjects come from his family's private museum at Chiclin, and not only their discovery but also our very knowledge of the cultures to which they belong are due largely to his own work. If it had not been for his kindness, it would not have been possible to illustrate the early periods in anything like an adequate way.

I am also grateful to the University Museum, Philadelphia, Pa. and the Musée de l'Homme, Paris, for permission to reproduce photographs taken from material or negatives in their possession. To Mr. Adrian Digby, Keeper of the Department of Ethnography, British Museum, I am much indebted for help in connexion with the photography of objects in the Department.

Dr. Irving Rouse of Yale University has kindly obtained permission for me to reproduce the Chavín carving shown in Figure 4, and Dr. J. H. Rowe of the University of California has been good enough to assure me that the drawing of Interlocking vessels forming Figure 10 may be reproduced.

I would like to express my gratitude to Mrs. Glyn Daniel for the personal interest she took in drawing many of the figures and the map.

My thanks are also due to Mr. L. P. Morley, the photographer of the Cambridge University Museum of Archaeology and Ethnology, for the skill and patience which he has expended on many subjects from that Museum.

It is fitting to end this introduction with a tribute to the memory of Wendell C. Bennett. He excavated in many different parts of Peru and Bolivia, and his knowledge, freely given to the world, was both wide and deep. His many friends will long remember a wise counsellor and a most kindly and cheerful companion.

G. H. S. B.

CHAPTER I

Introduction

WHAT WE MEAN by Ancient Peru is not quite the same geographically as the modern state of Peru, although the boundaries approximate to one another in some directions. Highland Bolivia is included in it, but the greater part of the lowland forest area east of the Andes, which now falls within its frontiers, is not. As so defined, Ancient Peru was a cultural area, the whole of which shared a common tradition of long duration, and it is often called by archaeologists the Central Andes.

There can be few regions in the world where a short journey brings the traveller into such variations in climate and topography as Peru. On the west is the coastal plain, one of the great deserts of the world, where there are miles of scorched rocks and crescentshaped sand dunes. Life would be impossible here were it not for the river valleys which cross it from east to west, where the ancient peoples irrigated an area greater than their successors ever did until quite recent times. To the traveller who flies over the coast, these valleys appear as a succession of narrow green belts amid great stretches of yellow and brown; they vary greatly in size though the larger ones are generally in the north. A short distance inland rise the foothills of the Andes, range upon range, and far above, on a clear day, may be seen one or other of the snowcapped peaks of the Western Cordillera. Many of the valleys are household words in Peruvian archaeology, among them being Chicama, Moche and Virú in the north, Chancay in the centre, and Chincha, Ica and Nazca in the south. In some cases, the valleys are separated, not only by desert strips, but also by rocky spurs, and the result is that the culture of each developed to some extent in isolation, though as time went on some tribes were able to subjugate their neighbours and add valley to valley,

Plate 3

particularly in the north, where the larger size of the valleys allowed powerful units to develop. It is important to realize that the water supply of a valley all came from a single source, the river, and that this, of necessity, imposed a high degree of unity on the inhabitants as soon as the population increased beyond the smallest scatter. As irrigation developed, it became necessary to organize the people, not only to construct and maintain the ditches but also to see that the water was fairly distributed. The consequence was, in several instances, the emergence of a highly centralized type of state. Although the topographical contrast between mountains and coastal plain is very great, the difference presented, in many cases, less of an obstacle to cultural diffusion than the deserts and rocks of the coast, although the peoples themselves must generally have retained their permanent domicile near the altitude at which they were born.

The mountain region, which forms the backbone of the area, is highly diversified. Below the high ranges, with their snow-capped peaks, are passes, high plains or *punas,* basins, and numerous river valleys, most of them steep and narrow. Small numbers of people can live in many places in the valleys, but there are only six areas which could support large groups in ancient times. These are, from north to south, the Cajamarca Basin, the Callejón de Huaylas, which is the basin that feeds the Santa River Valley, parts of the Mantaro River Valley, the Cuzco Basin and adjacent valleys, the high plains to the north-west of Lake Titicaca and the Bolivian Plateau to the south-east of it. The punas are generally covered with grass, and although they lie at such a height that, when the sun is off them, the cold chills the marrow of anyone accustomed to a lower level, they form ideal grazing grounds for the herds of llamas and alpacas which are such a valuable asset to the inhabitants.

The water supply presents a contrast to that of the coast. There are regular rains and multiple sources of supply are

Plate 2

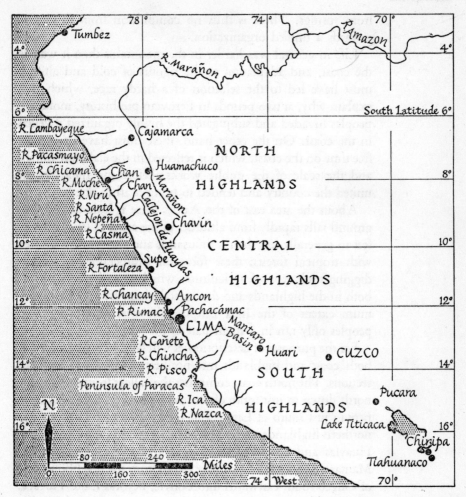

Fig. 1. Map of Ancient Peru.

available in each area. There is no exclusive dependence on
irrigation, although some of the terraces, which were formed on   Plate 71
the steep hillsides in order to extend the limited area available
for cultivation, were watered by stone-lined channels leading

from springs. There is thus no compulsion from this cause towards a unified organization.

Life in general was harder in the mountains than it was on the coast, and adaptation to the rigours of cold and altitude must have led to the selection of a hardy race, which may explain why, at two periods in Peruvian pre-history, mountain peoples invaded and subjugated the highly organized dwellers in the coast. On the other hand, there must have been more free time on the coast, which is reflected in the elaborate burials and the scale of the public works, before the Inca Empire united the country and tended to bring it all to one level.

About the area east of the Andes there is little to say. The ground falls rapidly from altitudes of the order of ten thousand feet to generally less than a thousand, and the earth is covered with tropical forests; these form an insuperable bar to the digging-stick type of agriculture, which was the basis of life both in the highlands and the coastal plain. Even at the maximum extent of the Inca Empire, the writ of the highland peoples only ran in a small part of the area.

For the purposes of description, it will be convenient to divide both coast and highlands into northern, central and southern sections. The north coast comprises the valleys from the extreme north down to just south of the Casma Valley, the centre from here to just south of Lima, and the south the remainder. The northern highlands cover the Cajamarca Basin, the Callejón de Huaylas and the intervening area, the centre comprises the Mantaro Basin, and the south extends from the neighbourhood of Cuzco south-eastwards into Bolivia, beyond Lake Titicaca. Parts of all these areas are virtually unknown archaeologically, but perhaps the worst gaps are in the central highlands and the extreme north, both highlands and coast. The most complete succession so far known is in the central part of the north coast, where the Virú Valley has been studied in detail, and a great deal of work has been done in the neighbouring Valley of Chicama.

It is well known that the Spaniards, after their arrival in the New World, found two areas which stood out from the others, namely Mexico and Peru. The difference between these areas and those which surrounded them was mainly political, since the peoples of Central America, Colombia and Ecuador were at much the same technological level as those of Mexico and Peru. Wherever natural conditions permitted, they depended on digging-stick agriculture, they wove, they made pottery, and they knew the same metallurgical processes. It is probable that the Peruvians surpassed all others in the excellence of their weaving, but the metal work of the tribes of parts of Ecuador, Colombia and the Isthmus of Panamá was as good or better than that of their more powerful neighbours. On the other hand, the peoples outside Mexico and Peru consisted mainly of small independent tribes, as for example, the peoples of the Coclé district in Panamá, who were divided into a number of tribes, each under a despotic chief. The chief exception is found in the highland basins round Bogotá in Colombia, where a number of related tribes, the Chibcha, controlled a large area at the time of the Spanish Conquest, but they seem to have fought among themselves a great deal, and in any case it is unlikely that they could have extended their dominion far outside their own highland area even if their progress had not been interrupted by the Europeans. The Valley of Mexico was occupied, in the last few centuries before the arrival of the Spaniards, by a number of related tribes. One of these, the Tenochcas, generally called the Aztecs, of Tenochtitlan on the site of Mexico City, had achieved what must have been a rather uneasy domination over the remainder when the Spaniards arrived, and had subjugated a considerably wider area to the extent of exacting tribute from the inhabitants. The Aztec Empire, as it is sometimes called, did not approach that of the

Incas of Peru, in size, cohesion, or thoroughness of organization. The latter, as we shall see, was a true empire with a
pyramidal organization culminating in an absolute hereditary
ruler, the Supreme or Unique Inca, to give him one of his
honorific titles, whereas the Mexican Montezuma, whom the
Spaniards regarded as the Emperor, was one of two almost
equal high chiefs, who were chosen by the tribal council, in
which the ultimate authority rested. The Aztec state was,
nevertheless, highly organized, their society showed a high
degree of specialization, and in Tenochtitlan, their capital,
they had an urban centre of great splendour.

Such in brief outline was the picture in the sixteenth century,
but, if we look back at earlier times, the same areas were always
in advance of their neighbours. The civilized area of Mexico
comprised, it is true, much more than the Valley of Mexico,
since it included pretty well the whole of the south and south-
east of the country and much of Guatemala and Honduras.
Both of the nuclear areas, as Peru and Mexico are sometimes
called, have, indeed, been more fully explored than the neighbouring ones, but this is largely due to the fact that they
attracted exploration because their archaeological remains were
more spectacular than those of other areas. It cannot be claimed
that much of America south of the Rio Grande has yet been
explored as fully as it deserves, nevertheless it is clear that future
discoveries can never challenge the pre-eminence of Mexico
and Peru.

THE HISTORY OF EXPLORATION IN PERU

Much of what we know about the Incas and the tribes under
them is derived from written sources, since some Spanish
writers and some like the Inca Garcilazo de la Vega, who were

of mixed Inca and Spanish blood, knew their civilization either at first hand or from their parents. The study of these writings, attempts to reconcile contradictions between them, and observation of the spectacular architectural remains of Inca times at Cuzco and elsewhere, have provided material for many publications, including Prescott's *History of the Conquest of Peru* and Sir Clements Markham's *Incas of Peru,* both of which are full of valuable information though deceptive in some respects.

It is not the object of this work to give a full account of Inca civilization, for which reference can be made to other sources, particularly J. H. Rowe's account in the *Handbook of the South American Indians (see* Bibliography, p.141).

Something has long been known of pre-Inca cultures from the numerous pots, pieces of fine textiles, and objects of gold, copper, wood and stone, which have been looted from the coastal graves and found their way into museums, but in view of the lack of written records of these earlier periods, the building up of any sort of chronology had to await the beginning of serious archaeology. This started when Max Uhle, the German archaeologist and anthropologist, began work in the nineties of the last century, and carried on a series of excavations during the next twenty years, first for the University of Pennsylvania, then, under the patronage of Mrs. Phoebe Hearst, for the University of California, and finally for the Peruvian Government. Much of his work was never published by him, but with the aid of his collections and notes at the University of California, A. L. Kroeber and others produced a masterly series of publications on his collections from various sites. Kroeber himself followed this up by an expedition to Peru in 1925 and 1926, under the auspices of what was then the Field Museum at Chicago, which resulted in several additions to our knowledge of various parts of the coast, and at the same time the Ecuadorian archaeologist, Jacinto Jijón y Caamaño, worked in the

neighbourhood of Lima. S. K. Lothrop, whose special contri,
bution to Peruvian archaeology is in the field of metallurgy, was
also working there in 1925.

By this time, largely owing to Uhle's work, we knew that in
all parts of the coast there were comparatively old cultures,
particularly Proto,Chimú, now called Mochica, in the north
and Nazca in the south, which were obliterated by the spread of
a highland culture with its centre apparently at Tiahuanaco, on
the Bolivian side of Lake Titicaca. Later, local cultures
emerged again on the coast, the Chimú in the north having
some features in common with its Mochica predecessor but the
others distinct from those which went before. These were soon
submerged in their turn by the spread of the Incas. Of the
earlier part of the succession, all that was known was the
existence of shell middens near Ancón, in the central coast,
which Uhle believed to be the dwellings of primitive canni,
balistic fisher folk, but which have since been recognized to
belong to the Chavín horizon. At this time it was also realized
that wide areas were united by the art styles, shown chiefly in
pottery and textiles, of Tiahuanaco and the Incas, and they
were called Horizon Styles.

Beginning as early as 1913, Julio C. Tello, the doyen of
Peruvian archaeologists, ranged far and wide over Peru, ex,
ploring the most inaccessible places and making large collec,
tions. This work he continued until his death in 1947, but
although he published several general schemes of development
of the Peruvian Cultures, he never gave the detailed evidence on
which they were based to the world, and it is to be feared that
much information died with him. Perhaps his chief contri,
bution to archaeology, and it is a very great one, is his recog,
nition of the importance and early date of the Chavín Culture,
of which the type site is a great temple at Chavín in the
northern highlands. For some years he and Uhle engaged in
a controversy about the origin of the Peruvian Cultures, Uhle

maintaining that all the main ones came from Central America by sea, while Tello was of the opinion that they all took their origin in the Peruvian Andes. The final answer has yet to be determined, but recent work has revealed surprisingly close relationships between Chavín and Central America, though many of Uhle's contentions will not bear critical examination.

In 1934 began a period of great activity with Wendell C. Bennett's expedition to Tiahuanaco, the first of a most fruitful series covering much of Peru and highland Bolivia. His work continued at intervals until shortly before his premature death in 1953, at about the time when the results of his last expedition to Huari in the Mantaro Basin were ready to go to press. In 1940 and 1941 a Columbia University expedition under Duncan Strong, one of Kroeber's associates in his earlier work, worked in the Central Coast, and among other sites investigated the great ruins at Pachacámac, where Uhle had worked before. After Strong had returned home, Gordon R. Willey continued the work of the expedition with excavations on Uhle's 'primitive' sites at Ancón and Supe, thereby increasing our knowledge of the Chavín horizon on the Central Coast.

In the meantime, Rafael Larco Hoyle and his family were working quietly in and around their estates in the Chicama Valley in the north coast. Among his discoveries in this and the neighbouring valleys is a representative of the Chavín horizon, besides two subsequent pre-Mochica periods, and he distinguished five successive stages in the Mochica itself. A number of useful publications bear witness to these and other discoveries, and not least among the family's contributions to knowledge are their magnificent collections housed in the Museo Rafael Larco Herrera on their hacienda at Chiclín, where many archaeologists and interested visitors have enjoyed their generous hospitality.

Immediately after the war of 1939 to 1945, a number of United States institutions, with the collaboration of the

Peruvian Instituto de Estudios Etnológicos under Dr. Luis E. Valcárcel and Dr. Jorge C. Muelle, launched the Virú Valley project, in which it was planned to survey the archaeology, human geography and ethnology of a self-contained area of manageable dimensions from the earliest time to the present day. The scheme was successfully carried through and most of the results have been published by the institutions concerned, with the consequence that we now have a complete, well attested sequence in one area, although we yet have much to learn about the total development of the cultures represented. Among those who took part were Bennett, Willey and Strong, whose earlier work has already been mentioned, Junius Bird, Clifford Evans, Donald Collier, and James A. Ford. At much the same time, John Rowe, of California, spent some years in Cuzco, where he investigated the chronology of the Inca period both in the library and in the field, besides excavating the first pre-Inca remains to be found in the region. More recent work includes another Columbia expedition under Strong, this time to the south coast, which has produced some important data, of which only a summary has yet been published, and an investigation by Henri Reichlen, of Paris, and his wife, of the region round Cajamarca in the northern Andes.

In spite of all that has been done, the general picture of Peruvian archaeology is still full of gaps, large areas have barely been touched, and there is still plenty of work to do.

DATING AND CHRONOLOGY

See *Bibliography*, Bennett, 1948

As a result of the Virú Valley work and that which went before it, it has become possible to formulate a series of developmental stages which, as a working hypothesis, have been applied to the whole Central Andean area, enabling us to think of it as a unit and greatly clarifying description. This scheme was first put forward at a conference held at the Larcos' museum at Chiclín in 1946, and further defined at one held in New York in the following year. An outline of the scheme will be given at this point, in order to clarify what follows, and further details will accompany later chapters.

The earliest inhabitants of Peru were a hunting people, generally called the Early Hunters. They were succeeded by the Early Farmers, a sedentary people whose dwelling sites are so far known only on the coast, where they lived by fishing, gathering of wild plants, and small-scale agriculture. After this began the Formative Period, divided into two stages, the first a theocratic stage to which the name Cultist is sometimes given, and the second characterized by diversity of development in different areas and by the introduction of new technical processes, called the Experimenter Period. According to our present knowledge, the Cultist Period is synonymous with the Chavín horizon, a name which will recur constantly in the following pages. After the Formative comes the Classic Period, characterized by the complete mastery of practically all the pre-Columbian crafts and technological processes, and the existence of some flourishing states, whence it is sometimes called the Mastercraftsman or Florescent Period. The Mochica and Nazca cultures, already mentioned, are among those assigned to this stage. The term Classic was first applied in the New World to a similar stage in Middle America, but its exact equivalence in time and in character to the Peruvian Classic is in some doubt. The post-Classic follows; it is a time when there were few technological developments, but a good deal of political evolution. It has three divisions; in the first, the highland culture associated with the name of Tiahuanaco spread over most of the coast, a movement probably accompanied by military force, and for this reason it is called the Expansionist Period. Then came the City Builder Period, associated, at any

DATE	TITLE OF PERIOD		NORTH	CENTRAL	SOUTH
				Coast	
1500	POST CLASSIC	Imperialist	Inca	Inca	Inca
1000		City Builder	Chimu	Cuismancu	Chinch
		Expansionist	Coast Tiahuanaco	Coast Tiahuanaco	Coast Tiahuan
500	CLASSIC	Mastercraftsman or Florescent	Mochica	Interlocking	Nazca
A.D.					
B.C.	FORMATIVE	Experimenter	Gallinazo or Virú	Negative	Necropol
500		Salinar or Puerto Moorin	White-on-Red	Caverna
1000		Cultist	Cupisnique	Coast Chavín	
1500					
2000	EARLY FARMERS		Early Farmers		Early Far
2500					
3000					
7000	EARLY HUNTERS ? Between 3000 and 7000 B.C.				

Fig. 2. Chronological C

Highlands

AR NORTH	NORTH	CENTRAL	SOUTH (Cuzco)	(Titicaca)	
Inca	Inca	Inca	Inca	Inca	1500
amachuco			Early Inca	Local cultures. Chullpa	
					1000
huanacoid (ajamarca)	Local Tiahuanaco		Local Pottery Styles	Decadent Tiahuanaco	
		Huari	Tiahuanaco		500
Cursive (ajamarca)	Recuay			Classic Tiahuanaco. Pucara	
					A.D.
				Early Tiahuanaco	B.C.
Chavinoid (ajamarca)	White-on-Red		Chanapata	Chiripa	500
	Chavín				1000
					1500
					2000
					2500
					3000

rate in the coast, with the building of great urban centres, many of them associated with the Chimú Culture, already mentioned. Finally came the Imperialist Period, the time of the spread of the great Inca Empire.

Until a few years ago, the only dates available for Peruvian archaeology were some for the Inca Period, derived from study of writings at the time of the Spanish Conquest. For the earlier periods there was nothing but intelligent guesswork. The next step was taken by Junius Bird who, in the course of his work on the Virú Valley project, made some estimates of the rate of accumulation of middens and natural deposits, which gave dates of about 3000 B.C. for the beginnings of agriculture and over 1000 B.C. for the introduction of pottery. Subsequent developments have shown that these are of the right order of magnitude. For the later periods, James A. Ford made estimates based on the relative thicknesses of deposit in the Virú Valley, but these suggest the telescoping of the latter part of the succession to what many archaeologists consider an unreasonable extent. An attempt has also been made to date some Mochica artifacts found buried in the guano on various islands off the coast in the last century, using estimates of the rate of accumulation of the guano and the depths at which the objects were found, but the figures were based on nineteenth century records since the guano was long since quarried away, so there is some doubt about the reliability of the evidence. A date in the ninth century A.D. was indicated for certain Mochica artifacts.

After this came radiocarbon dating, which has put the earlier part of the sequence on a much firmer footing. At the XXIX International Congress of Americanists in New York in 1949, Dr. W. F. Libby of Chicago announced the first date to be measured for the American continent, namely, about 800 B.C. for the beginning of the Chavín Period on the coast. Dates which have since been obtained are a good series for the

See *Bibliography*, Johnson, 1951

Early Farmer deposits in the Chicama Valley, with a few for the Mochica and earlier periods in the same region, and a very few for the south coast. No post-Mochica dates have been measured. At the other end of the scale, Rowe's studies of post-Conquest records strongly support the date of A.D. 1438 for the beginning of the Inca expansion.

In sum, the early part of the succession, the Early Farmers and the beginning of the Chavín Period, is soundly dated and the dates are generally accepted. The same is true of the Inca expansion. The situation for the intermediate periods is not so satisfactory, since the radiocarbon dates are few and surprisingly early, so that their acceptance makes it necessary to spread the latter part of the succession over an unexpectedly long time. They conflict seriously with Ford's estimates for the Virú Valley. This is best illustrated by the Mochica Period; radiocarbon indicates that it is unlikely to have ended in the Virú Valley after about A.D. 300, or 500 at the latest, whereas Ford puts it as late as A.D. 1150. Some archaeologists find both these extremes difficult to accept and compromises have been suggested, but pending further measurements, I propose to accept the radiocarbon dates with due reservations, and place the Mochica Period vaguely in the first half of the first millenium A.D., though it may have begun up to three centuries earlier. The great need at present is for more measurements, not more guesses. Most of our dates so far come from the north coast, where we also have the most complete succession, but other areas can be correlated with it with the aid of horizon styles and general development.

Before going on to deal in detail with the growth of the Central Andean civilizations, a few words must be said about their nature and the characteristics which are shared by the whole area during a long period of time. The essential pattern took shape in the Formative Period, but its full flowering came later.

In the first place all were based on intensive agriculture, with no more elaborate tools than the digging-stick, clod-breaker and hoe. Many plants were cultivated, the chief being maize, which gives good crops up to a height of about 12,000 feet, but only ripens in a few places above. At greater altitudes its place is taken by another grain called quinoa, which is hardier. The potato is a native of the area, and assumed a great importance throughout the highlands. Irrigation was an essential feature, and it was accompanied in the highlands by terracing, which extended the cultivable area and resisted erosion. Fertilizers were used, namely bird guano and small fish heads in the coast, and llama or human dung in the highlands. Food was preserved by drying or freezing, a well-known example being the dehydration of potatoes by repeated exposure to frost and sun, sometimes followed by pressing, which produces an insipid substance called chuño; this is still much eaten at the higher altitudes. Dried meat, called charqui, whence the name 'jerked' meat, was prepared by a similar process. The narcotic coca, which was grown in the valleys on the eastern slope of the Andes, was chewed with lime everywhere in the area, and its use on the coast is one of the factors which proves the existence of trading contacts with the highlands at an early date.

Plates 2, 58, 63, 70

In the highlands, the herding of llamas and alpacas, the domesticated American cousins of the camel, was second only to agriculture in importance, but they do not live permanently on the coast, although they were often taken there and their skeletons are commonly found in archaeological deposits. The alpacas were prized particularly for their wool, and the llamas were used as pack animals (although they will carry little more than 100 lb), their meat was eaten, and their hair was some﹣times used for coarse textiles. The dog and the cavy, or guinea﹣pig, were the only other domestic animals, the latter being the chief source of meat in Inca times. Hunting was always sub﹣sidiary, and organized hunts became an upper﹣class occupation in later times, but there is evidence for the hunting of deer, pumas and foxes, and the wild representatives of the llama family, the guanacos and vicuñas.

The basic social unit was a village group consisting of a number of related families under a headman, owning their lands in common, to which the Quechua name of *ayllu* was applied when the Inca conquest spread that language outside the Cuzco area. On this were superimposed complex types of society, with marked distinctions of class and function.

An important characteristic of all Central Andean peoples was great manual skill associated with very simple apparatus, a feature which they shared with other South and Middle American peoples. Their weaving was unsurpassed and is particularly characteristic of the area; they applied most of the known techniques, using both cotton and wool, with great dexterity on a simple back﹣strap loom. Pottery was skilfully modelled and painted, producing vessels of great artistic merit, but the potter's wheel was unknown. Gold, silver, copper and their alloys were worked by a variety of processes, and the production and working of bronze were finally mastered. Among the useful metals, the most obvious absentee was iron, which was unknown anywhere in America, except for rare instances derived from meteors. Many other materials such as wood, basketry and stone were skilfully worked, and were used, where appropriate, on a large scale for massive building as well as for the smallest ornaments. As an example, it is only necessary to cite the fine masonry of the Incas, with stones between which a knife blade cannot be inserted. It appears that everyday products, such as domestic pottery and textiles, were made by the members of each family, but that the finer cere-monial goods, which, so far as our evidence goes, were generally made to be buried with the dead, were the work of specialists.

The later cultures of Peru, those of the Incas and their immediate predecessors, possessed most of the features that are regarded as the hall-marks of a civilized community in the Old World, particularly fully efficient food production, urban centres, a formal political state, public works, and classes and hierarchies. The advanced cultures of the Mastercraftsman Period possessed most of these features, with the apparent exception of urban centres, though recent work in the Nazca area seems to have revealed a considerable city. On the other hand, all the New World cultures lacked certain features which accompanied the growth of civilization in the Old. Iron and the potter's wheel have already been mentioned, and to these are to be added any sort of draught animal and wheeled transport. Above all, Peru lacked written records, even the picture-writing of Middle America, and although there must have been strong oral traditions, supplemented by mnemonic devices, such as the system of knotted strings called the *quipu* and perhaps others, the catastrophe of the Spanish Conquest must have been a great blow to these traditions. The result is that our knowledge of the intangible features of Inca civiliza-tion, literature, laws and so on, is very imperfect, and we are cut off almost completely from those of pre-Inca ones.

Great interest has been aroused in recent years by Heyerdahl's voyage across the Pacific on the Kon-Tiki raft, and by his theory that Peru played a major role in populating Polynesia. It is unquestionable that wooden rafts were in use in ancient Plate 50 times on the Peruvian coast, since centre-boards and steering sweeps like those used on the modern balsa rafts of Ecuador and on the Kon-Tiki are found in graves, particularly on the southern part of the coast. It is not known whether the rafts themselves were built of the light balsa wood now used, and it may not have been available before the Incas conquered part of what is now Ecuador. The prevailing opinion is that they were used for coastwise traffic, as the Spaniards observed when they arrived in the region, although Heyerdahl's discovery of potsherds of Peruvian north coastal types on the Galápagos Islands shows that they could travel a considerable distance from the coast. This, however, is a very different matter from colonizing Polynesia, and the theory that the Peruvians did so does not commend itself to the majority of serious students either of Oceania or of Peru.

At no time and in no place has archaeology escaped the attentions of cranks, and Peru is no exception. The idea of Perry that the civilization of ancient Egypt was transplanted lock and stock, with the possible loss of the barrel, to Peru has been largely forgotten in the light of increased knowledge, but the ruins of Tiahuanaco, in the Bolivian highlands, were still provoking the wildest speculations less than a decade ago. This site dates from some time in the first millenium A.D., and can certainly not be appreciably older, but by considering it in isolation from the general development of Peruvian culture, invoking irrelevant considerations of astronomy, and ignoring the most elementary facts of geology, a writer has seriously claimed that it is a quarter of a million years old and that it was overwhelmed by an ocean tide some 14,000 feet high!

CHAPTER II

The Early Hunters

LITTLE IS KNOWN of the earliest men who lived in Peru, but some light can be thrown on them by giving an outline of early man elsewhere in the American Continent. The first men to arrive in the New World must have come from Asia across the Bering Straits, at a time when all men lived by hunting and gathering wild plants. There were times during the Ice Age when this route was blocked by ice, but there were others when it was clear, although the ice elsewhere still locked up so much water that sea-level was low and the straits either narrower than they are now or quite dry. Large mammals, like mammoth, mastodon and an extinct species of bison, found their way across and down into America, making tracks through the grass-lands which provided them with food. Man in search of meat followed them, and evidence of his presence in the shape of pressure-flaked stone projectile points and other stone tools is found in many parts of the United States, especially the Great Plains, in Mexico and elsewhere. An early type of point called the Folsom has been dated in the United States at about 8000 B.C., but it is known that other types are older, since they have been found in deposits underlying Folsom ones and separated from them by signs of an advance of the ice. One such advance has been dated to a period just before Folsom, but its duration is uncertain, and all that can be said at present is that the pre-Folsom men must have been in America by at least 10,000 B.C. and probably earlier.

Excavations by Junius Bird at the opposite end of the continent, in Southern Patagonia, have shown that man was hunting sloth, horse and guanaco in that region by between 6000 and 7000 B.C., so he must have been in Peru before that. His route into South America could only have been across the

Isthmus of Panamá, whence he could have followed the Cauca or the Magdalena Valley into the Colombian Andes. From here, his most reasonable way southward into Peru was to follow the highlands, since tropical forests on either side in Colombia and Ecuador would be a bar both to him and to the animals which he hunted. In Peru, there are rock shelters near Huancayo in the central highlands, which may belong to this period. They contain flaked stone points and tools such as scrapers and blades, and they lack pottery in a region where it is abundant, so it is reasonable to regard them as pre-ceramic rather than merely as non-ceramic survival of later date. In the desert north coast, Rafael Larco and Junius Bird have found workshop sites where pressure-flaked points and other imple-ments were made, at La Pampa de los Fósiles and other sites between the Chicama Valley and that of Pacasmayo to the north of it. The points generally have a short stem, and may be long and lanceolate, but are more commonly more or less tri-angular. Some were made in a rather unusual way from a thin layer of tabular chert of the thickness of the implement, so all that was necessary was to trim the edges into shape. Roughly made side scrapers and blades are also found. Although there are no stratigraphical indications of age, the presence of pressure flaking in a region where it does not occur at a later date makes it virtually certain that these sites are to be ascribed to bands of these early migrants, who left the bleak highlands for the warmer climate of the coast, at a time when the climate was doubtless wetter than it is now. Although it is likely that other early hunter sites will be found, they are bound to be sparsely distributed, since the population at this time, consisting as it did of nomadic bands, must have been extremely small.

Recent work by Duncan Strong in the south coastal area, which has only been published in brief outline, has shown the presence of sand-blasted stone tools, including flaked projectile points, obsidian scrapers and knives, and many obsidian flakes, in low shell heaps in the Bay of San Nicolas, just south of Nazca. They are accompanied by shellfish, and bones of fish and sea-lions, and seem to point to a stage when the hunting peoples realized the possibilities of food obtained from the sea, and could therefore settle down without practising any form of cultivation.

CHAPTER III

The Early Farmers

ALONG THE PERUVIAN COAST are several sites which were the dwelling-places of a people very different from the early hunters. We do not know where they came from, but we do know that they are the first link in a chain of development which went right up to the time of the Spanish Conquest in the sixteenth century. The earliest signs of their presence can be dated at about 2500 B.C. and we do not yet know anything about what went on in Peru between the first appearance of the early hunters and this time. The sites are middens, mounds formed by the accumulation of debris round the dwellings, and in at least one of them the dry climate and the lack of ground water has allowed all the perishables to be preserved, so that we have a complete cross-section of the belongings of the people. There is one site near Pacasmayo, two in the Chicama Valley, one in the Virú Valley, and some, about which little has yet been published, just south of Lima and in the neighbourhood of Nazca.

One of those in the Chicama Valley, the Huaca Prieta, has been carefully excavated by Junius Bird, whose work in Patagonia and elsewhere has already been mentioned, and this has given us most of the information we have about the period. It lies at the mouth of the valley, on the right bank of the river, and is about 40 feet high. The valley must have looked rather different from what it does now; there was no irrigation, the vegetation must have been confined to naturally wet areas along the meandering river, and there may well have been swamps and lagoons along the lower reaches. The Quechua word Huaca, belonging properly to certain classes of objects of worship, is applied nowadays to any ancient mound or ruin or even to pottery vessels from graves, and the designation Huaca

35

Prieta, or Dark Huaca, refers to its unusual dark colour, which is due to the organic debris consequent on its being a midden and not an artificial pyramid like so many of the huacas along this coast. It had a bad name among the local 'huaqueros' or grave-robbers, who came to leave it severely alone because it never yielded any of the pots which they sought, but when Bird was looking for possible pre-ceramic sites, Rafael Larco called his attention to it, with remarkable results.

The midden is some 12 metres or 40 feet thick and it has given a consistent series of radiocarbon dates from carefully collected samples, perhaps the most reliable application of the method yet carried out. The dates range from about 2500 to 1200 B.C., giving an accumulation rate of rather under a metre a century. The people lived mainly on the harvest of the sea; they collected shellfish, and since these include deep-water mussels they were probably good swimmers, and they caught fish in seine nets, which had floats made of bottle-gourds and sinkers made from cobble-stones with a hole pecked through. Similar nets are still used in the district by men who wade into the sea at low tide, so their use does not necessarily imply the presence of boats. The bones of a few marine mammals, namely sea-lions and porpoises, are found, but no land animals, and there are no hunting weapons. The other source of food was plants; wild plants were gathered, and a few were culti-vated, including squash, gourds, beans, chile peppers, and various tubers and roots, but maize, the great staple of later times, was quite unknown. Cotton was extensively used, and is presumed to have been cultivated. It has given rise to a good deal of speculation, since some geneticists believe that American domestic cotton contains an Asiatic component which, they say, must have been introduced by men crossing the Pacific in boats. Whatever views about trans-Pacific voyages we may hold, 2500 B.C. is an excessively early date for them to have occurred. The bottle-gourd is likewise believed by some to be of Old

World origin, but it may be suggested that enough attention has not been paid to the possibility that both plants were distributed naturally to the New World, under suitable climatic conditions in Tertiary times.

Fabrics, bags and fishing nets were made from cotton and a bast fibre derived from a species of milkweed. The fibres were spun by hand and are extremely irregular in thickness; no regular spindles and no spindle whorls have been found. The heddle was unknown and fabrics were made by hand, twining being the predominant process in about three-quarters of the fragments examined. In a small proportion, the wefts were darned in to produce a warp faced cloth similar to those made with a heddle, but this process is nearly always used in combination with twining, and the two may even appear in a single pick of weft. Bone needles, which may have been used in the darning, are among the finds on the site. Ornament was produced almost entirely by warp manipulation, sometimes combined with a limited use of colour, namely, the natural white and brown shades of cotton, plus a blue dye and sometimes a red pigment rubbed either into the threads or the finished product, though this is very fugitive. The effects include warp stripes and occasional warp float patterns, mostly very fragmentary, in the woven pieces, and transpositions of warp, to produce zigzag effects, most commonly in the twined pieces. The latter can be used in combination with colour, since the transpositions can be done in such a way as to bring alternate warps diagonally across their neighbours, so that one only of each pair is seen on the surface; if the warps alternate in colour, it is then possible to produce patches of a single colour on the surface, while the others are hidden behind. This technique, in combination with twining, is quite characteristic of the period and is never found again throughout the long tradition of Peruvian weaving. None but rectangular fragments have been found, some as small as five inches square, and some up to five

feet by four feet, but none can definitely be identified as garments, although some could possibly have been used as shawls.
Rush mats were similarly made by twining, and so were
baskets, but coiled basketry was not made. Among single
thread techniques, figure-eight looping was used to make nets
and bags. For knotted nets, the knot used was the cow-hitch,
which continued to be used in later times and is still widespread in South America. It is worth observing that it is not
found in Polynesia, though it should occur there if the islands
had been populated by people coming on Kon-Tiki rafts from
South America. Bark cloth occurs in small quantities, which
is a curious feature since it is a material associated rather with
the tropical forest than with this coast, where there are no trees
with suitable bark.

As has already been indicated, the inhabitants of the Huaca
Prieta and similar sites had no pottery. They seem to have
cooked by roasting on hot stones, or by boiling water in gourd
containers by throwing hot stones (pot boilers) into them. The
only stone implements are crude, percussion-flaked scrapers and
blades, in no way resembling the pressure-flaked points of the
early hunters. If the exceptionally dry climate had not preserved the perishable materials, few artifacts apart from these
tools and the net sinkers would have been preserved in the
lower part of this deposit, and we should have had a totally
false idea of the culture of the people.

Subterranean houses, consisting of single rooms of various
shapes, generally oval, lined with cobble-stones, and roofed
over at ground level with wooden or whalebone beams covered
with stones and mud, were found in the upper part of the
midden. Similar ones, lined with rectangular mud bricks,
called in Peru *adobes*, are found on the Virú Valley site, where
stones are not available in the immediate neighbourhood. The
earlier graves at the Huaca Prieta were simple pits, but the later
ones were similar to the rooms. There were few grave goods—

perhaps a cord bag containing a few leaves and dried flowers, and in one case a chewed quid, which is suggestive because in modern times a chewed quid of coca is reckoned to be a cure for some ills such as kidney trouble and toothache. At any rate the germ of the idea that the dead could carry something out of this world, which was expressed so dramatically in the elaborate burials of later times, was already present.

I have referred to these people as the Early Farmers, but

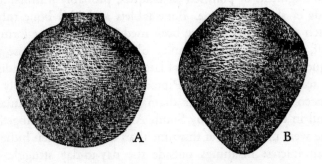

Fig. 3. Domestic pottery of the earliest type from the north coast, belonging to the Early Farmer stage after 1200 B.C. and the Chavín Period. Plain red or black ware. The height of such jars is from about 1 foot to 1 ft. 8 in.

perhaps a better name would be the Early Gardeners. Their agriculture can only have been on an extremely small scale, and there is no evidence for domestic animals, though doubtless they had the almost universal dog.

About 1200 B.C., some additions to the equipment of the people were made, without altering materially their way of life, and for this reason I prefer to class these people still with the Early Farmers rather than with the subsequent stage, as some writers have done. The most important new feature was pottery, but one of its chief advantages, namely, its use for cooking, was not at first grasped by all the inhabitants and pot boilers

Fig. 3

continued to be used for a time. The pots were simple jars, with an ovate profile, and the only ornament consisted of applied fillets of clay, which were either notched or pinched into a wavy form. The colour ranged from dull red, through dark brown to black, and its variability indicates that oxygen con׳ trol in firing was very imperfect. Other pottery artifacts were stamps, either flat or of the roller type, probably for making designs in paint on the body, and fragments of figurines. There were fragments of polished jet plaques, probably mirrors, and beads of shell and bone. Bone tablets and bird bone tubes, which are believed to have been used in taking some form of snuff, were also found; similar objects for this purpose are frequently found in deposits of later periods, and snuff made of the seeds of a tree called Piptadenia, or less commonly of tobacco, as an intoxicant for shamans, or merely as a stimulant, is still in use among many South American tribes. Altogether there were more signs at this time than there had been hitherto of an interest in things outside the day׳to׳day struggle for existence. There were also developments in building methods and houses were built above ground of adobes of various forms. The earliest of these were cylinders set vertically, some of them solid and some built up from thin discs, with the interstices filled in with clay, but later walls were built from conical ones, laid on their sides in two rows, with the points interlocking.

For all this information about the Early Farmers, we are indebted to Bird's excavations in the Chicama Valley, supple׳ mented by those of Strong and Evans in Virú, but more should soon be learnt from the sites recently discovered by Strong on the coast near the Nazca Valley in the south. So far, we only know that they are deep shell middens of early date, and that the lower levels appear to lack pottery and to contain textiles and plants similar to those found in the Chicama Valley.

See *Bibliography*, Bennett, 1948; Strong and Evans, 1952

CHAPTER IV

The Formative Period

THE NAME Formative was originally coined to describe the early stages of civilization in Middle America, but it has been adopted in Peru to cover cultures on much the same level. In both cases, they were the first steps in the development of the full flowering of the ancient American civilizations, differing from them in degree rather than in kind. The process began earlier in Middle America than it did in Peru, since agricultural peoples, settled in villages and making good pottery, were already established in Mexico by about 1500 B.C., and they grew maize, a plant which gives such good returns for the labour spent on it that there is much free time available for activities outside the production of food. The importance of maize in the high civilizations of America can scarcely be exaggerated, since it has been calculated that a Maya Indian in Yucatan can grow enough of it to support himself and his family, without domestic animals, by working for 48 days in the year. This figure must vary in different places, and there cannot have been so much surplus time in the early days of agriculture, but it gives an idea of the potentialities of the plant.

THE EARLY FORMATIVE OR CULTIST PERIOD

Maize had appeared in Peru, together with an elaborate form of pottery for ceremonial use and a religious cult which required imposing buildings, by about the ninth century B.C. and it probably arrived somewhat earlier, say 1000 B.C. All the known sites of this period belong to some form of the Chavín Culture, of which the north coastal aspect is sometimes called

Cupisnique. There is reason to believe that the new features were introduced by an immigrant people. The older inhabitants continued to live on and near some of their original sites, where their presence is shown by the persistence of the old types of utilitarian pottery, but the newcomers imposed their religious system on them. Food obtained from the sea was still important at this time, and some settlements, which have left large middens, were still on the sea-shore. Others were inland along the margins of the river valleys, but the central parts of the valleys, which later became so important, were still unoccupied, probably because the farmers were still unable to cope with the scrub and marshes which bordered the rivers themselves. Middens at Ancón and Supe, in the central coast not far north of Lima, are a considerable way from any cultivable land, and in the case of Ancón the distance amounts to 10 kilometres, but the proximity of the sea must have outweighed this disadvantage. Modern Peruvian Indians make light of long distances on foot, and their predecessors probably felt the same.

Fig. 3, A, B

In the Virú Valley, the only area where settlement patterns have been seriously studied, the population was small and the sites few. Little is left of the houses except the rough stone foundations, set in mud, of some small groups of rectangular or irregularly shaped rooms scattered at random. A pot in the form of a house shows a rectangular, gabled building, with thin walls but thicker foundations, and a thatched roof. The walls of these buildings were probably of adobe or cane. Subterranean houses, similar to those of the earlier period, but lined with adobes instead of cobbles, were still constructed in the Huaca Prieta in the Chicama Valley.

See *Bibliography,*
Willey, 1953

It is unlikely that irrigation had developed to any extent even by the end of the period, and cultivation must have been done in small clearings in exceptionally favourable spots, not necessarily very near the habitation sites. In addition to maize, the new plants included peanuts, alligator pears, warty squash and manioc. The people possessed dogs, since the desiccated remains of a small brown one were found in the cemetery at Supe. They also had llamas, which were almost certainly domesticated, since their bones were found at Supe and the remains of sacrificed animals were found on a ceremonial site in the Virú Valley. Their presence proves communication with the highlands, since they do not live permanently on the coast, and the evidence is supported by the occasional use of their wool in textiles in the later part of the period.

Relatively few textiles of this time have been preserved, and most of them are of cotton. The overwhelming majority are rectangular pieces of some kind of plain weave, with variations made by crossing single warps with a pair of wefts and vice versa, or by crossing pairs of warps with pairs of wefts. The commonest patterns are coloured warp stripes, which mostly seem to be based on the natural browns and whites of the cotton, and there are also weft stripes and tartan-like combinations of both. Angular patterns, such as interlocking steps, frets, and hollow rectangles, were produced by brocading or by building up patches of different colours after the manner of tapestry, although true tapestry, in which the wefts hide the warps, is rare. The patches of colour were joined by interlocking the adjacent wefts or by passing them round a common warp, or were separated by kelim slits, features which were all common in later tapestries. At Supe were found a few remarkable designs in the shape of a head combining condor and feline characteristics in typical Chavín style, and carried out in true tapestry technique. It is rather surprising to find tapestry with cotton wefts, since it is difficult to cover the warps with them, and it was much commoner for wool to be used in the later periods. Another type of textile was gauze, but examples are very rare. Loom weaving was clearly the normal process at this time, and twining appears to have gone entirely out of fashion, although it was by far the commonest way of making basketry. Unlike those of the Early Farmers the threads used were evenly spun, and pottery spindle whorls were used.

What little evidence we have suggests that clothing was scanty. The textiles found in graves are merely rectangular shrouds, and no clothing has been identified under them. One pot found by Larco in a north coast cemetery depicts a man

Fig. 4. The Feline God, with snake head appendages. Incised design from stone frieze slab at Chavín. Length about 3 ft. 3 in. (After Bennett.)

Plate 4

wearing a breech clout and a close-fitting headgear, and another which represented a nursing mother is not altogether clear but it shows that the upper part of the body was bare except for a veil-like head-dress falling down the back. There is some indication of body painting, in the shape of stamps made of pottery, found in graves.

We must go on to consider the ceremonial centres, the religion they existed to serve, and the art which adorned them. The principal object of worship was a feline god, of which the

Fig. 4

prototype must have been either the puma or the jaguar, or

perhaps both. The jaguar lives only in the tropical forests, but the puma is found all over South America in both highlands and lowlands, so on the whole it is the more likely of the two to have impressed itself on the imagination of the highland and coastal peoples.

By comparison with the ordinary settlements, some at least of the religious buildings were large and imposing, but there were no large concentrations of population round them. It has been suggested that the actual building of the temples was done by a comparatively small number of skilled masons, and that they were assisted in the collection and preparation of the materials by large numbers of people who gathered from time to time for religious festivals. Andean Indians have always been very much addicted to making pilgrimages of this kind in historic times, the shrine at Copacabana in Bolivia being a well-known instance, and it is reasonable to believe that this habit has persisted from early times.

The most notable of the centres was that at Chavín de Huántar, which has given its name to the Chavín Culture. It lies on a tributary of the Marañon River, just east of the watershed bordering the Callejón de Huaylas in the north highlands, and consists of massive rectangular platform-like buildings, ranged round a central court and faced with alternate courses of thick and thin dressed stone blocks, into which are tenoned massive human heads, many of which have feline tusks. The buildings are honeycombed with galleries and chambers on two or three levels, connected by stairways and ramps.

Many stone carvings come from this site, all of them being distinguished by feline features in some form, chiefly fangs and claws. One group consists of slabs with incised designs, mainly from a fallen frieze which formerly encircled the buildings, and besides complete felines, conflations of felines with other animals in the shape of condors and snakes with feline fangs,

Fig. 4

45

claws or markings are found on them. A most remarkable example of rather a different type is the tall stele known as the Raimondi stone, now in the National Museum at La Magdalena Vieja, near Lima, which bears a standing figure with a feline face, holding an elaborate staff in each claw-like hand, while from the head projects a monstrous appendage facing upwards and consisting of a series of fantastic snouts with feline fangs and snakes projecting on either side. Within one of the galleries of the building, Tello discovered a standing stone shaped more or less like a prism tapering downwards, and carved with a tusked feline face and other features.

Pottery has been found on this site, and it generally takes rather simple forms, of which the most typical is the open, flat-bottomed bowl, though bowls of other forms and narrow-mouthed jars or bottles are also quite common. More elaborate *Plates 7, 8* forms, like the stirrup spout, which will be described in connexion with north coastal sites, are rare. The ware is monochrome, red, brown or black in colour, and it may be decorated by incision, finger-nail impressions, a series of fine punctuations *Plate 5* produced by rocker stamping, brushing, or applied strips. The designs produced by these processes are commonly geometrical, such as solid triangles and rectangles, or curvilinear, in which case they may be parts of life forms which cannot be recognized on fragments. The ubiquitous dot and circle design is also found. These designs may be emphasized by shading, cross-hatching or rocker stamping. The variability in colour is due to lack of uniformity in the oxygen supply in firing, but the vessels are nevertheless hard and well fired.

Isolated finds of stone sculpture related to the Chavín style are found in various parts of the north highlands, but the most important site in that region outside Chavín itself is Kuntur Wasi in the upper part of the basin of the Jequetepeque River. Adequate reports of it are not available, but it is known that it is a triple-terraced pyramid crowning a hill-top, and that it formerly supported some form of temple. Some of the carvings found near it are related to those of Chavín, and Chavín type pottery is also reported. Gold ornaments with hammered re-poussé decorations and turquoise have been found in graves there, but it is not clear whether they are contemporary with the Chavín material. Potsherds of generalized Chavínoid character have been found in small quantities in the lowest levels of stratigraphical tests in the Cajamarca Basin, just over the watershed to the east of the Jequetepeque drainage, but they are decorated by red and white painting as well as by incision and it is therefore very probable that they belong to a slightly later development.

The most extensive discoveries of the Chavín horizon in the north coast are those made by Rafael Larco in the Chicama and neighbouring valleys, to which he gave the name Cupis-nique, after the small valley which yielded his first finds. Most of his material comes from cemeteries which he has excavated, and its richness indicates that many of the graves were those of important people. The graves were pits of various shapes, rarely lined with rough stones, and the bodies were generally buried in a flexed position, lying on the back or on one side. They were accompanied by grave goods, particularly stirrup-spouted jars, a form which is rare on Chavín sites elsewhere, and which may well have been made specially for burial. The stirrup spout has a long history in the north coastal area, and, apart from two interruptions, is found there right up to the time of the Spanish Conquest; it is accompanied by the flat base, and the presence of these two features distinguishes this area from the southern part of the coast throughout the archaeolo-gical sequence. Cupisnique stirrup spouts are distinguished from those of later periods by their massive character. The jars themselves are very variable in shape, ranging from spheroidal forms which may bear incised designs, sometimes including feline fangs and eyes, to elaborately modelled representations of

Plates 4, 7, 8

Plate 8. See also Plate 5.

47

human beings, animals, fruits and other objects, some of which were made in moulds. Plate 6, which presumably represents the face of an old woman, is a vivid illustration of the strength of the modelling.

Other grave finds in this region include stone plates and bowls, jet mirrors, shell and turquoise pendants and beads, and bone spatulae and rings, most of them adorned by carving which represents feline faces or fangs, thus testifying to the strength of the cult. Many of the graves contain little bags full of red paint composed of clay with traces of mercury and lead compounds, and when the flesh decayed this coloured the bones red, which at first led to the erroneous belief that the burials were secondary. Secondary burial, in which the bones are placed in their final resting place after the decay and removal of the flesh, is quite exceptional in Peru at any time, in fact our present knowledge suggests that it was not practised at all, although it occurs quite frequently on the Ecuadorian coast, and is one of the many features which differentiate the archaeo-logy of the two regions.

No Chavín buildings have been excavated in the Chicama Valley, but some foundations are believed to belong to cere-monial buildings of the period. In the neighbouring Virú Valley, the lower parts of the rough stone walls of a simple rectangular temple containing two low platforms, with a stair-way leading up to one of them, were found. This was chiefly interesting for the burials of four llamas which were found in or near it. All except one either had the remains of rope harness in place, or had their legs tied together with it, and there is little doubt that they had been sacrificed.

Farther south, in the Nepeña Valley, there are remains of more imposing buildings at Cerro Blanco and Punkurí. The first has stone walls bearing relief decoration in clay, painted brick-red and greenish-yellow, representing eyes and feline fangs of Chavín type, and is associated with incised and polished black pottery. That at Punkurí is a terraced platform with a wide stairway, on which stands a feline head and paws, modelled in the round from stone and mud, and painted. At its feet is the burial of a woman who is believed to have been sacrificed. Higher up are clay-plastered walls made of conical adobes, bearing incised designs of Chavín character.

The next valley to the south, that of Casma, has remains of rather similar character. At Moxeke and Pallca are terraced, stone-faced pyramids with stone stairways. Moxeke has niches containing clay-plastered reliefs made of mud, stone and conical adobes, showing felines, snakes and human beings of Cha-vínoid character, painted in white, yellow, black and red. Pallca is associated with dark-coloured monochrome pottery, and a bone spatula carved with a Chavín-type snake head with feline features has been found there.

In the same valley, at Cerro Sechín, is a rectangular building consisting of a series of superimposed platforms with a central stairway, on either side of which, at the bottom level, stands a row of unshaped flat stelae alternating with smaller stones, which are more or less square in form, and which were set in pairs or threes on top of one another. All bear remarkable incised or low relief designs. Most of those on the stelae are standing men, wearing loin-cloths and truncated conical hats and carrying staves or clubs, but a few lack the hats and weapons and have a limp or depressed appearance (one may be meant to be cut in half) as though they had been vanquished by the other type. Those on the smaller stones are severed human heads in profile, like head-hunters' trophies, the earliest example of a feature common in Peruvian art. One of the stelae bears a double column of such heads, seen full face. Some Chavín pottery has been found on the site, and although the carvings have no feline features and are not similar to Chavín types, small objects from various parts of the coast bear designs which link the two styles, and Sechín must be of similar age.

Plate 9

Plate 10

D

The sites in both Nepeña and Casma are very imperfectly studied, and the succession is not sufficiently well known for it to be possible to say where Sechín belongs in the Chavín Period, but the opinion of most archaeologists is that it is earlier in date than Moxeke and Pallca. Some writers have conjectured that there may be some connexion between the carvings of Sechín and a row of stones bearing low relief figures called Los Danzantes at Monte Albán, in the Mexican state of Oaxaca. In view of other evidence, there may well be a contact between Mexico and Peru at this time, but it cannot be said that there is any close resemblance between the carving of these two sets of figures.

To the south of Casma, no unquestioned ceremonial sites have been found, but there are remains of dwelling sites in the shape of shell and refuse mounds at intervals on the coast as far south as the neighbourhood of Pachacámac, south of Lima. Of these, the only ones which have been studied in any detail are those at Ancón and Supe, which have already been mentioned. An important cemetery has recently been found by Peruvian archaeologists near Ancón, and this has yielded many artifacts of wood, bone and stone, as well as baskets, pottery and cotton textiles. The pottery is similar to that of Chavín itself, consisting mainly of bowls and flasks, whereas the stirrup spouts so characteristic of Cupisnique are very rare. The stone objects include pestles, cylindrical mortars with engraved designs, and tetrapod plates; among those of wood are bowls, rectangular dishes and boxes, and there are bone awls and spatulae. Many of these are carved with feline designs of Chavín character.

With one possible exception, no metal is found at this period except gold. A thin crumpled fragment of hammered sheet gold comes from Supe, and a little simple hammered gold work is reported from Virú, but away to the north, at Chongoyape in the Lambayeque Valley, some more elaborate objects have been found. There are head-bands, cuffs, ear spools, tweezers, rings and other things, with elaborate repoussé Chavínoid designs; welding and soldering were employed in their manufacture. There are also a few objects of silver. It is believed that the Chavín religion and art style survived in this area to a later date than it did farther south, and that this is the explanation of the relative complexity of the metal-work. Some support is given to this theory by the association of pottery of Chavín character with later types in graves at Pacatnamú in the Jequetepeque Valley.

Two reasons have been given for the local variations in the expressions of the Chavín Culture. The first is that there was local specialization, with emphasis on stone-carving at Chavín de Huántar, elaborate pottery in the Chicama area, metallurgy in the far north, and so on. The other is that the variations are largely due to differences in time. The duration of the period is unknown, but evidence of increasing elaboration within it has been found in the Virú excavations. As has been already said, the peculiar site at Sechín is probably earlier than Moxeke and Pallca in the same valley, where the polychrome painting of the reliefs may well indicate an approach in time to the later Mochica Culture, of which polychrome frescoes are a known feature. Kuntur Wasi also is believed to be later than the type site of Chavín de Huántar. Both causes probably played their part in producing the differences, but it will not be possible to do more than speculate on the extent of their influence until detailed studies, like those carried out in Virú, are made in many more areas.

There is, then, evidence of the Chavín Culture spread over a wide area in the northern highlands and the north and central coast, but so far it has not been found elsewhere in Peru. It is united by the presence of similar pottery types, and by evidence of a religion of animal worship, in which the cult of a feline god held the foremost place. There are a number of ceremonial centres which show a considerable variety in detail, and each seems to have been the nucleus of a group of scattered settle/ ments, but there is no indication that the centres were united by any sort of political organization. Weapons are not common; flanged and spiked stone mace/heads and polished stone lance/ heads occur in the graves of the Chicama region, the spear/ thrower was in use, and a single long palm/wood bow was found at Ancón, but some at least of these must have been used for hunting. Fortifications are unknown, so fighting can hardly have amounted to more than small/scale local raiding, and the carvings at Sechín indicate that head/hunting may have played some part in this. With a small population in a few scattered settlements, there cannot have been any of the competition for land which so often provokes wars.

An important question which remains is, where did the bearers of maize, ceremonial pottery, and feline cult come from? Tello upheld the view that the Chavín Culture came to the coast from the highlands, with its ultimate origin in the Amazonian forests, but recent work has shown that it is most unlikely that any high culture ever developed or survived for any length of time in these forests. Others have suggested that the art style at any rate developed on the coast, but Bird's demonstration that Chavín pottery appeared abruptly with maize in the Chicama Valley has given strong indications that the whole complex was probably imported from a source farther afield.

Clues to where its origin may be have recently been found far away from Peru. At Tlatilco, near Mexico City, is a site belonging to the Formative Period, which shows many specific resemblances to Chavín, particularly in the pottery. It has been stated that some sherds from the two areas are so alike in ware and decoration that it would be hard to distinguish them, and those highly distinctive features, the stirrup spout and zigzag rocker stamping are found in both. The practice of fronto/ occipital head deformation in both areas may be more than

a coincidence, and the representation of felines was a characteristic feature of the Olmec Culture of Mexico, which had
a great influence on the art of the Tlatilco site. The site has not
been very precisely dated, but it is believed to belong some-
where in the middle of the Formative Period of Mexico, and
to be approximately of the same age as the beginning of the
Chavín Culture. It must not be thought that the cultures of the
two areas are identical, and attention must be drawn to two
main differences. As far as our present imperfect knowledge
goes, there were no buildings in Mexico which were comparable in elaboration with those of the Chavín Culture at the
time when Tlatilco flourished, and certainly none at Tlatilco
itself. In common with other Mexican Formative sites, Tlatilco
is distinguished by an abundance of pottery figurines, whereas
these are virtually lacking in the Formative of Peru.

South of Tlatilco, there are large gaps, but some evidence to
link the two areas is beginning to appear. In Honduras, at the
Playa de los Muertos in the Ulua Valley, there is a site whose
pottery resembles that of Tlatilco very closely. This also is a
long way from Peru, but a very recent discovery on the Baba-
hoyo River on the coastal plain of Ecuador gives promise of
further links. On this site a deep cut by Dr. Clifford Evans and
his wife, and Señor Emilio Estrada, has yielded pottery with
many of the features common to both the Mexican and Peruvian areas.

THE LATER FORMATIVE, OR EXPERIMENTER PERIOD

The Later Formative Period was one of technological innovation and variety in expression in different areas. The overwhelming preponderance of feline motifs in art had disappeared,
which suggests that the widespread feline cult had suffered a

setback, though examples of a modified form are found in the south coast. There is also evidence for the persistence or revival of the cult in both north and south coasts in later times, though it no longer had a virtual monopoly. Ceremonial structures in the form of pyramids occur in Virú, but nothing comparable in elaboration to Sechín, Punkurí and the rest has yet been found. A modelled jar from the Chicama Valley, in the form of a circular building, with a flat roof supported by walls con, sisting of stepped pillars surmounted by a decorated pierced frieze, probably represents an adobe temple or shrine.

The definition of the limits of the period is bound to be somewhat arbitrary, and as knowledge increases some cultures may be shifted into the succeeding Classic stage, just as it has already been suggested that some Chavín manifestations may have persisted after the Cultist Period, but in general it seems to be a valid division. There is insufficient dating evidence at present, and it cannot be said with certainty that all the Experimenter Cultures, which are more widely distributed than those of the preceding period, are contemporary. Although there is great diversity in different areas, the north and central coast from Chicama to near Lima, and the Callejón de Huaylas in the north highlands, are linked by two styles of pottery painting, which are regarded as marking two horizons, an older White-on-Red horizon and a younger Negative one. The following are the developments ascribed to the Experi, menter Period:

The Salinar Culture, belonging to the White-on-Red horizon in the Chicama Valley.

The equivalent of Salinar, called Puerto Moorín, in the Virú Valley, where it is followed by the Virú or Gallinazo Culture, of the Negative horizon, most of which is placed in this period.

A White-on-Red horizon in the Callejón de Huaylas. This is followed by the Recuay Culture, with negatively painted pottery, which is generally placed in the succeeding Classic Period.

Representatives of both horizons in the central coast.

The Paracas Cavernas and Paracas Necropolis Cultures in the south coast.

The Chiripa and perhaps the Early Tiahuanaco Culture in the south highlands, near Lake Titicaca.

The Chanapata Culture, near Cuzco, in the south highlands.

In addition, some little-known painted pottery styles found in the Cajamarca Basin in the northern highlands probably belong to this stage.

There was an improvement in agricultural methods at this time, and evidence from the Virú Valley shows that irrigation developed rapidly in the later part of the period, although it is doubtful if it was practised at the beginning. In the highlands there are indications of stone-faced terraces, perhaps the fore-runners of the irrigated terraces which are such a striking feature of the landscape in some of the narrow Andean valleys, and which greatly extend the cultivable area. It seems also that a number of new plants were cultivated. Among these, a grain called quinoa, which is of great importance in modern times at altitudes too great for maize to ripen, was found by Bennett in a stone bin at the south highland site of Chiripa. Coca, the leaves of which are still chewed by Andean Indians as a nar-cotic, has been found in a south coastal grave, and other new-comers are a variety of bean and a sterile hybrid like a cucumber, which can only be propagated by means of cuttings.

For evidence about houses and villages in the coast we are mainly dependent, as before, on the work which has been done in the Virú Valley. In the Puerto Moorín Period, the founda-tions, of rough stone or conical adobe, of two main types of settlement have been found; one consists of scattered irregularly

See *Bibliography*, Willey, 1953

shaped rooms, and the other of haphazard clusters of rooms, which tend to be more or less rectangular because they touch their neighbours. An open-fronted house, with a sloping roof supported on beams with a central post, is represented on a Salinar pot. There are also a few hill-top redoubts, containing houses and a pyramid within a stone wall, which suggest that there was at times a necessity for look-outs or defences, although there is no evidence for warfare on any considerable scale.

In the Gallinazo Period, sometimes called Virú, because its main development is in the Virú Valley, there were great developments. The dwelling sites were what are described as agglutinated villages, that is to say large groups of adjacent rooms, with successive stages piled one on another like a Near Eastern tell, and they may be built initially on a platform mound. Some of these are associated with pyramids, and were therefore religious and probably administrative centres also. They were built of adobes which varied in form, the conical ones of earlier times having given place first to balls and then to rectangular ones, while the material was sometimes used in the massive form called tapia. The main irrigation canals seem to have developed in this period, and some cultivation plots connected by narrow, looped channels can still be seen. The number and distribution of the sites suggest a great increase of population, made possible by irrigation, which in its turn imposed the necessity for a closely integrated society, since an elaborate system of canals can only be maintained and the water shared out by strict control. In the final stage of the Gallinazo Period, both population and irrigation system seem to have reached the maximum, and imposing strong points, containing adobe pyramids and dwellings defended by walls, a development of the older redoubts, were perched in commanding positions on peaks overlooking the valley. This last stage was contemporary with part of the Classic Period in the Chicama Valley, and is properly placed in that period.

The utilitarian pottery in the Virú Valley gives us further information about the population. From its earliest appearance it developed gradually in type, without sudden changes, right through the Formative Period, and this indicates that the same people remained there, although they increased in number. The simple jar with rounded base, ovate profile, and plain constricted mouth, continued, and the other main type in Puerto Moorín times was very similar, with a wider mouth and

Fig. 3B

 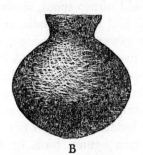

A   B

Fig. 5. A, B. Domestic jars of the Experimenter Period, in the Virú Valley. A. Puerto Moorin stage. B. Gallinazo stage. The size of these and similar types of the same age is very variable. They range from about 2 ft. down to about 8 in. in height, but most appear to exceed a foot.

low, everted lip. The chief changes which occurred were better mixing of the paste and more uniform oxidation in firing, producing thin, even-textured ware of a uniform brown or red colour. In Gallinazo times, the gradual change continued; for example, the jars developed a more globular outline, and some had a high flaring collar. These were the pots which were in domestic use, but there were other types to which brief reference has already been made, which were designed for religious or ceremonial purposes and are found almost exclusively in the graves. The decorated wares of the Chavín Period, outstanding among which are the Cupisnique types, belonged to this class

Fig. 5A

Fig. 5B

and those of the Upper Formative in the same region are related to them but show considerable change.

Some details must now be given of the various Experimenter cultures. Salinar, in the Chicama Valley, is known chiefly from funerary pottery belonging to the White-on-Red horizon, which resembles the plain pottery only in the paste and the oxidized firing. Like those of Cupisnique before them, the vessels are elaborately modelled and take many forms, including the old stirrup spout, as well as jars with a narrow, tube-like neck and a strap handle, and globular jars with a symmetrical arrangement of a sloping spout balanced by a modelled figure, the two being connected by a flat, bridge handle. The first whistling jars belong to the latter type, and the figure holds a spherical whistle, which sounds if air is drawn through it by pouring water out of the jar. In later times, the whistle is generally hidden within the figure, or a head which takes its place. Human figures, birds or animals are frequently shown on Salinar vessels, and more often than not they are perched on the top rather than forming the body of the jar, but the modelling is not so naturalistic as in Cupisnique. The human figures are lively little caricatures, with little or no clothing, sometimes shown in erotic attitudes, which are, unlike most of those depicted on vases of the Classic Period, invariably natural. Simple white lines, or triangles, sometimes filled with dots, are painted direct on the red surface of some Salinar jars. The burials with which these pots are found are generally in an extended position, in a simple grave, which may be covered with slabs or poles, and in some cases they had a round or oval gold plaque in the mouth, an interesting custom which is found also in later times. Salinar is the same as the Puerto Moorín Culture of the Virú Valley, of which various features have already been described.

Little can be said about the White-on-Red horizon in the Callejón de Huaylas and the central coast, in both of which it

Plate 11

Plate 12

is only known from trial excavations. The highland sites, near Chavín and Huaráz, have yielded grave pottery which is mostly in the form of bowls with slightly rounded bases and flaring sides, painted with simple designs such as triangles covered with dots or groups of parallel zigzag lines. The excavations in the Chancay Valley in the central coast produced huddled burials, protected by parts of large storage jars, which had been wrapped in textiles and in one case had a metal mask. This mummy bundle type of burial belongs to a south coast

Fig. 6. Mammiform jar. The type is characteristic of the Central Coast in the Experimenter and Classic Periods. Height varies from about 6 in. to 2 ft.

and south highland tradition, which does not spread to the north until later times. The commonest pottery types are incurved bowls with a pair of loop handles, and mammiform jars with a collar, carelessly painted with white dots, dotted triangles or broad white zones on red, or in some cases one half white and the other red. The general simplicity of the forms links this area with the north highlands and distinguishes it from the Chicama region, as in Chavín times.

Fig. 6

The Negative horizon is represented in the Virú and Santa valleys by the Gallinazo or Virú Culture, which is found so sparsely in the Moche and Chicama valleys that Larco believes that the graves there must belong to migrant groups from Virú.

Although its later stages must be regarded as Classic, it is convenient to speak of it here. Something has already been said of
the buildings, irrigation canals and plain pottery, and a word
must be added about the funerary pottery. Stirrup spouts and
Plates 13, 14, 17 other modelled vessels are frequent, particularly a spout and
bridge type with a tapering spout. Most of these vessels are red
in colour and some are decorated with negative designs in
black, produced by painting a pattern in wax before firing and
covering the whole with black, so that when the pot is fired the
wax comes off and the design stands out in red on a black
See Plates 26–8 ground. Negative painting is widespread in Peru and only in
a limited area can it be regarded as marking an horizon. It is
uncertain where it was invented, but the oldest examples are
probably in the south coast, and in the north it is most likely
that it spread from Virú up into the highlands, whence it may
have moved northwards into Ecuador and Colombia. Little
can be said about its occurrence in the central coast, since it is
only known from sherds found in the deeper refuse levels at the
important ceremonial centre of Pachacámac, south of Lima.
The Virú vase shown in Plate 14 is one of the few feline
representations in this period, and that in Plate 17 represents
a warrior holding club and shield sitting in a small raft made
Plate 18 of a bundle of reeds, such as fishermen still use on the Peruvian
coast. It illustrates the emergence of militarism and the warrior
class, and raises the question of the use of the sea for transport.
Balsa wood rafts were used for long voyages in Inca times and
sailing rafts were in use on the south coast at an earlier date, but
the roads from valley to valley were the controlling factor in
coastal communications until the arrival of the Spaniards, who
depended on the sea and neglected the roads. In aboriginal
times, the domination of one valley by another depended on the
existence of a road, and the variety in the coastal cultures during
the Experimenter Period shows that few of the valleys were
connected in this way.

In the south coast, the main developments so far known are in the Nazca and Ica valleys and the Paracas Peninsula, but we can only have a one-sided view of them until Professor Duncan Strong's work is fully published. Up to the present the cultures of this area have been chiefly known from the rich burials found by Tello on the arid peninsula of Paracas, whither the dead must have been carried from the valleys where they had lived. There are two main types called Paracas Cavernas and Paracas Necropolis.

The Cavernas type of cemetery consists of deep dome-shaped rock-cut chambers, which may be up to 25 feet below the surface, approached by a narrow, vertical shaft with steps cut in the walls, above which is a wider, cylindrical antechamber lined with stones. They contain many mummy bundles, in one case 55, in which the body sits with the knees up to the chest, wrapped in many layers of cloth. These are mostly of plain weave or gauze, with little colour except two-colour stripes. The skulls are generally flattened artificially, and frequently trepanned, extensively and sometimes repeatedly. The reason for this is unknown, but it has been suggested that it was a consequence of fighting with the stone-headed clubs which are found in many of the graves; this suggestion does not carry much conviction, since clubs are by no means confined to this time and place, whereas the practice of trepanation is more frequent and extensive here than anywhere else, and some religious explanation is more probable. Whatever the reason, the victims survived the operation, and not once only. Among the rich grave goods are highly characteristic pottery types, including heavy open bowls with simple negative designs in orange and dark brown, plain or incised black bowls or jars, and bowls and jars painted after firing in black and rich red, yellow and green resinous colours separated by incised lines. The jars take many forms, which include the double spout and bridge, and the variety in which one spout is replaced by a head, and

Plate 15
Plate 16

Plate 21

the designs include feline faces, which is one of the chief reasons why some writers have argued that Cavernas belongs to the Chavín horizon, although the style is distinct. All, both bowls and jars, have the rounded base which is characteristic of the south coast. Very rare are strange figurines, similarly decorated but in pale colours. A cemetery at Ocucaje in the Ica Valley has yielded similar pottery from shallow, rectangular graves, also human skulls cut vertically in half, the front half retaining the hair and skin. Houses and other structures of adobe and wattle and daub have also been found at Ocucaje.

The other Paracas type, Necropolis, consists of rectangular pits of various sizes, unroofed and filled with mummy bundles and sand, from which over 400 bundles have been taken. These contain a body sitting with the knees up, often in a basket, and wrapped in many layers of superb textiles, many of which are covered with intricate embroidery in vivid colours, reds, blues, yellows, greens, browns and others, representing grotesque figures, monsters, birds, animals and other designs, arranged with great artistry. They take the form of mantles, shirts, loin-cloths, turbans and other garments, and a single bundle may contain many examples of each, which are quite unworn and were presumably made specially for burial. They are distinguished by the use of embroidery for ornament, in contrast to the weaving techniques like tapestry and brocade which were common in other Peruvian cultures. There are fragments in many museums which give a good idea of the colouring and the nature of the designs, but the figures dressed in complete garments in the National Museum in Lima make a sight not easily forgotten. The skulls of these mummies are highly deformed in a manner different from those of Cavernas, with the result that they are long and narrow, but trepanation is relatively rare. The pottery includes shapes similar to the Cavernas ones, but it is generally lighter in construction and cream or brown in colour.

Plate 19

Plate 20

The burials were those of honoured and important people, and the preparation of their graves and all that were in them must have occupied much time and effort. We know little about the living on whom this burden lay, although Strong's excavations have shown that some of them lived in the Nazca and Ica valleys, where he has found remains of wattle and daub houses, and evidence of three stages of development. The correlation of Cavernas and Necropolis with these is not simple, but it appears that the earliest stage has negatively painted pottery and other Cavernas features, and that the second has elements of both cultures. As far as it goes, this supports the usual view that Cavernas precedes Necropolis, but this order is not universally accepted.

See *Bibliography,*
Bird and
Bellinger, 1954

The Formative cultures of the south coast are in a tradition distinct from those of the north, since they have different pottery shapes, polychrome painting of pottery, advanced development of textiles, full clothing in breech clout, shirt and mantle, and different burial customs. Even the feline motifs are in a different style. The origin of this tradition is obscure, and so are its relations with Chavín and the subsequent northern cultures, but the development of clothing perhaps points to an immediate source in the cold highlands.

The Experimenter Period in the south highlands is represented by Chiripa, a site excavated by Bennett on the Bolivian shore of Lake Titicaca. This was a village of fourteen rectangular houses standing round a circular court. They were built of rectangular adobes on a foundation of stones packed in clay, and were thatched with grass. The cold was resisted by two features, namely, double walls with storage bins between the two thicknesses, and vertical slots for the reception of sliding wooden doors. The most usual pottery vessel is a thick bowl with flat base and vertical sides, painted with simple geometrical designs, like steps, in broad yellow strokes on a red slip, which, like the whiteonred of the coast, suggests the tentative beginnings of painted decoration. It is probable that the early stage at the famous site of Tiahuanaco in the same neighbourhood should also be classed as Experimenter, but it will be convenient to discuss the site as a whole under the heading of the Classic Period. (*Note:* Bennett originally regarded Chiripa as later than the Tiahuanaco Classic Period, but in his later publications he abandoned this opinion, having become dissatisfied with the evidence.)

At Chanapata, on the outskirts of Cuzco, J. H. Rowe did some trial excavations on a site where a road section revealed rough stone-walling and potsherds of non-Inca types. He found a semi-subterranean room, bounded by retaining walls, and some huddled burials in circular or oval pits, with no grave goods. Abundant potsherds were found in the excavation, and the same types can still be collected on the site. They are hard and mostly brown, dull red or black, either plain or decorated by incision, stabbing or appliqué ornament, or by partial burnishing. There are collared jars, flat plates and bowls of various shapes, including flat based ones, with vertical or flaring sides. Some finer, painted wares are present, but they are in two colours only, as in other cultures of this period. The designs are very simple, and include circles and stepped forms in white on red, or red on buff.

There were few advances in metallurgy during the Experimenter Period, but a gold-copper alloy is known from Salinar and the central coast, and pure copper is found at Cavernas and Chiripa.

CHAPTER V

The Classic Period

THE CLASSIC PERIOD in Peru is marked, not only by the full development of technical processes, which has suggested Bennett's alternative name of Mastercraftsmen, and by flourishing art styles, but by the establishment of highly organized and aggressive states. This feature, which is not characteristic of the Classic of Middle America, may well have been due to the topography of the coast, where dependence on irrigation imposed a strict organization on the inhabitants of the valleys. This does not account for similar social developments in the southern and central highlands, because highland basins, in contrast to the coastal valleys, generally had more than one source of water, so there was not the same compulsion towards unity. There is as yet no satisfactory explanation for what happened in this highland region, unless it was due to copying of the coast, but the centre of development is still not absolutely certain, so it is perhaps premature to seek an explanation for it. The chief expressions of the Classic Period are to be found in the north and south coast, and in the south and central highlands, and subsidiary ones are known from the north highlands and the central coast. The extreme north of both coast and highlands, and much of the central highlands, are still little known.

Agriculture was fully developed, with elaborate irrigation patterns filling some but not all the coastal valleys, and it is probable that the terraces of the highland valleys were greatly extended. The full range of pre-Columbian plants was known and cultivated, and grave finds and representations on pottery suggest that many of them were added during this period, including such well-known vegetables and fruits as the potato, the sweet potato, the papaya and the pineapple.

Practically all the aboriginal techniques of weaving were known, and both cotton and the wool of the llama and the alpaca were extensively used. Textiles are better preserved in the south coast than they are in the north, but it appears also that elaborate weaving was a speciality of the south coast at all times, and part of the south coast tradition. Tapestry, brocade, double cloth, gauze, warp stripes and weft stripes are all common, and twill was known, but the embroidery so characteristic of Paracas Necropolis was out of fashion. No textiles of this time have been preserved in the wet climate of the highlands, but spindle whorls and statues representing clothed figures give indirect evidence of their manufacture. A simple type of belt loom was used for many of the processes and its use is proved by the painting on a remarkable pottery vessel of this period from the north coast, which shows a number of women working under the direction of a formidable-looking matron. Actual examples of later periods are known from coastal graves. Elaborations of this sort of loom must also have been in use. The twills which have been found indicate the use of three heddles instead of one, and modern analogies suggest a similar arrangement for making double cloth. The width which can be woven by a single weaver on such a loom does not exceed about 2 ft 6 in., and the discovery of fabrics up to 17 feet wide was a puzzle, until some modern Peruvian weavers provided the clue by remembering that their mothers used to work wide looms of the same type in teams, sitting side by side.

Mechanical aids, however, meant little to the old Peruvians, and manual dexterity was all-important. Many processes like braiding were carried out entirely by hand, and others like the making of triple cloth and tapestry depended little on normal loom processes, a fact which is particularly apparent in the case of a rare piece of tapestry from Nazca, in which beads are strung on some of the warps. Another hand process consisted in building up patches of warp of different colours on scaffold wefts on a frame. The threads of adjacent patches are inter-locked with one another, and each patch has wefts of the same colour darned in, and in their turn interlocked with one another at their edges. The scaffold wefts can then be removed, and if an unfinished piece had not been found it would have been difficult to guess how it had been made. The whole process calls for the greatest skill and care in the maintenance of constant tension, otherwise the fabric would become hope-lessly distorted.

The fine quality of many of the fabrics depends on the selection and spinning of the fibres, at which the Peruvians were adept. A measure of this is given by the fact that a tapestry, of post-Classic date it is true, has as many as 500 two-ply wool wefts to the inch in some places, whereas the best that Medieval Europe attempted was about 100. Dyeing was another impor-tant factor, and it is surprising to realize that the great range of colours found at Paracas was produced by combinations of only three vegetable dyes, indigo, red and yellow to orange-brown, with the natural colours of cotton and alpaca wool, using where necessary an alum mordant. Needlework involved the use of many varieties of stitch, and although knitting was unknown an identical effect was produced with a single needle in making borders of three-dimensional birds and flowers at Nazca and Paracas. Most garments were made by joining rectangular pieces, and tailoring was unknown, but some were woven to shape. Thus it was possible to widen the shoulders of a shirt or the ends of a loin-cloth by spreading the warps at the appropriate place, and inserting extra ones between them where there was room. The end beams of a loom could be set farther apart at one side than at the other, and extra wefts carried across part only of the web, which would produce a fabric longer at one side than at the other. Two forms of tie-dyeing were in use in Ancient Peru, but, so far as we know, they date from post-Classic times, so they will be described later. Many

of the work-boxes used by Peruvian women have been
preserved; they are mostly of wood covered with twilled
basketry and contain, among other objects, balls of wool and
cotton, and numerous thin, pointed spindles, some of them
wound with thread, with small, delicately decorated whorls of
wood or pottery. These were suitable for spinning with one end
resting in a bowl, which was the ancient custom, rather than
falling free according to modern practice in the Andean region.

In metallurgy, it is believed that all the pre-Columbian
processes and alloys were in use, with the exception of the
making and fashioning of bronze. Metals were used chiefly for
making ornaments, such as collars, ear spools, nose ornaments
and false faces for mummy bundles, but in the Mochica Culture of the north coast, which seems to have specialized in
metallurgy just as the southern area did in textiles, useful objects
such as blades for digging-sticks, mace-heads and lance-points,
were made of copper. Gold, silver and copper, and alloys of
gold and copper and silver and copper were all worked. It is
believed that gold was obtained mainly from placer deposits,
but there is no evidence about the sources of silver and copper.
There is some reason to believe that both were smelted from
ores in post-Classic times; in the case of copper this could be
done fairly easily, and the corpse of a miner, with his basket full
of a powdery copper ore, which was found in a collapsed shaft
in North Chile, is one of the most popular exhibits in the
American Museum of Natural History. On the other hand,
both metals occur in a native state, and it is reasonable to
believe that this was their source in the early days of their use.

In working the metals, gold was hammered and embossed as
in the past, and the same processes, in combination with
annealing, to soften them when hammering had made them
hard and brittle, seem to have been applied to the other metals.
Casting was employed, and it is probable that the *cire-perdue*
process was known. Gilding seems to have been done by the

Plate 40

Plate 45

See Plates 47–9

application of gold leaf, but the details of the process are not known. It may also have been done to gold-copper alloys by leaching out the copper on the surface with organic acids, hammering and burnishing, but this method was commoner in Ecuador and Colombia. Gilding by the use of mercury was not known. Pieces of metal were joined by welding, that is by heating and hammering, and by soldering, which was probably done by covering the junction with powdered copper salt mixed with gum; on slow heating, the gum would char and reduce the salt to metal, producing a local patch of gold-copper or silver-copper alloy of lower melting point than the metal which was being joined. Objects made partly of gold and partly of silver are known, and it has been suggested that they were made in two stages by the *cire-perdue* method.

Although each area in Peru had reached a similar techno-logical level, and each had imposing buildings and public works, the art styles differed radically from one another, and at least in the north and south coast they continued the older traditions. This is sufficiently exemplified by the ceremonial pottery, which in the north coast was distinguished by natural-istic modelling, stirrup spouts, flat bases, and few colours, and in the south coast by round bases, double-spouted jars and polychrome painting, with figure modelling far less frequent and far more stylized than in the north.

The Mochica Culture of the Pacasmayo, Moche and Chi-cama valleys represents the Classic Period over much of the north coast. It was in part contemporary with the Gallinazo Culture of the Virú Valley, and late in their history the Mochica people invaded Virú and subjugated it, extending their conquests beyond it to the Santa, Nepeña and Casma valleys. The name Mochica is taken from the language which was spoken by the Chimú people in the same area, and these their predecessors may or may not have spoken it. It is a con-venient name, and has superseded the old terms Proto-Chimú

Plates 22–5

Plates 30, 32

NORTH COAST
Mochica Culture

and Early Chimú, because these tended to cause confusion by obscuring the fact that there was a break between Mochica and Chimú. The name is preserved in the modern valley and village of Moche.

Like other peoples at this time, the Mochica depended largely on agriculture for their living, but fishing naturally continued to play its part, as it always did on the coast. Fish were caught with barbless hooks and nets, both from the shore and from the reed boats already mentioned. Judging by representations on pots, hunting was rather an upper-class sport than a general means of supplementing the food supply, since richly attired men are shown throwing darts from spear-throwers at deer surrounded by nets into which they had been driven. Men are also depicted shooting birds with a blow-gun, but this must have been an individual occupation.

The Mochica occupation of the Virú Valley resulted in some changes in the distribution of sites, but dwellings, temples and strong points do not seem to have altered very much in type. Plain rectangular adobes were the usual material. The vast adobe pyramids called the Huaca del Sol and the Huaca de la Luna in the Moche Valley date from this period, and so do many pyramids and other works in Chicama. Among these is a great earthern aqueduct at Ascope, which is about 50 feet high and carries a canal for nearly a mile across the mouth of a dry valley. It was intact until it was accidentally breached during the abnormal rainy season of 1925, and it remains an extremely impressive sight, which gives some idea of what the Mochica were capable of. A canal in Chicama, 75 miles long, which still irrigates some fields near Chan Chan, the Chimú capital, is believed to date from this period.

While the existence of these great works and the extensive irrigation patterns implies closely-knit organization, we know little about its details, apart from what can be gleaned from scenes and people represented on the ceremonial pottery. Gorgeously attired individuals, sitting on thrones or carried in litters, must in some cases be important chiefs, and others, who may wear masks, doubtless represent gods or priests impersonating gods. An important burial from the Virú Valley, which will be described later, seems to be both warrior and priest attired and equipped to represent a god. Combinations of this sort, and numerous representations of warriors and weapons, show that the organization was not exclusively theocratic, as it seems to have been in the Early Formative Period, but that there was a strong secular side to it also. Varieties in type and elaboration of costume, and the advanced condition of the crafts, point to a specialized as well as a stratified society. Women are depicted plainly clad in a kind of long shirt with a cloth covering the head, and they do not appear in the elaborate ceremonies painted on some of the pots, so they are generally believed to have had a subordinate place, but there must have been excep-tions, since one burial in Virú had grave goods of considerable importance.

Plate 24

The domestic pottery continued to change gradually, and the most popular type in Mochica times was a wide-mouthed red jar or deep bowl of globular outline, while collared jars de-creased in popularity. Grey wares, fired under reducing con-ditions, are present in increasing quantities. As before, the ceremonial pottery differed in a marked degree from the utili-tarian wares, and took the form of the well-known red and white modelled type to which reference has already been made. This is a thin, well-fired ware, red in colour, to which is added a slip, either white or partly white and partly red. Details are then picked out in red on the white, or less commonly in white on the red. Late in Mochica times a third colour, black, was sometimes added to a small extent. The vessels are of many shapes, of which the most frequent is some form of stirrup spout and others include bell-shaped bowls with ring bases and flasks with flaring collars, which may be either globular or elaborately moulded. More or less hemispherical bowls, double vessels, and a peculiar flattened bowl, known as a dipper, with a constricted mouth and a conical handle projecting from the side like that of a frying pan, are also found. The plain forms are decorated either with pressed relief or with painted designs, which may take the form of elaborate scenes; some of the best of these are found on the bell-shaped bowls, where they generally occupy a broad zone on the inside, adjacent to the margin. Some vessels show a combination of these techniques, which may also be combined with moulding.

Larco has established five successive stages in the development of Mochica pottery, and it will suffice to say here that they are distinguished by such features as the form of the stirrup and the nature of the decoration; for example, Plate 25 shows an early form of stirrup, which has something in common with its Cupisnique ancestors, and an early form of pressed relief, and Figure 7 shows a late form of stirrup and a late type of painted decoration. In general, elaborately painted scenes and carelessly executed painting are signs of a late date, and so is black paint.

Most of the vessels were made in two-piece pottery moulds, such details as stirrup spouts being added afterwards. The moulds themselves were made from a solid or thick-walled model, and, being porous, they absorbed moisture from the castings which therefore shrank away from them and could easily be removed when dry. This method results in the production of near duplicates, but they are seldom exact since minor differences in decoration and even in form were introduced while finishing the vessel.

The naturalistic modelling and the elaboration of the painting makes these vessels singularly informative sources of evidence about the life of the people. Some head jars are so expressive and so carefully modelled as to be clearly portraits, and the faces would not look strange among the inhabitants of the remoter coastal villages at the present time. Others could well be caricatures. Several varieties of male dresses are shown, a usual type being a square-cut shirt, like a modern poncho sewn up at the sides, under which the breech clout can just be seen. In other cases there seems to have been rather a longer

Fig. 7. Late Mochica stirrup-spouted jar with geometrical painting. Height 10 in.

under-shirt with a skirt reaching to the knees, sometimes girded with a sash, with a short poncho-like shirt with short sleeves over it. Another variety is a mantle worn over a shirt. Some of these garments display elaborate geometrical borders and other decorations, sometimes heraldic in effect; on one jar there is a warrior with a tabard-like shirt gyronny red and white, along-side one with his shirt divided bendwise into red and white

Fig. 8

73

halves, the white one sprinkled with red dots. No shoes or sandals are shown, but the legs may be painted to resemble socks. Most men are shown wearing ear ornaments, which generally take the form of spools which may have large circular ends. Examples are known of gold, silver, copper, wood and bone, with inlays of shell, turquoise and other materials. There was great variety in head-dresses, which in some cases were simple skull-caps, but were often of great elaboration and included reconstructions of birds and animals, semi-lunar copper blades, bushes of feathers, and many other features, as varied as the crests on any medieval roll of arms. The warrior with the gyronny shirt has a conical helmet with a kind of mantling, both similarly adorned, surmounted by a copper blade. All head-dresses were secured by a band under the chin. The nature of the head-dress must have been related to the rank and function of the wearer, though it is only possible to suggest what a few of them represent. One group, who are believed to be messengers, wear only a breech clout and a head-dress which includes an animal head and a long appendage trailing behind, and they are seen speeding along and carrying a bag which may contain beans. Beans bearing dots, lines and other designs are, indeed, shown on these and other scenes, and Larco, who has found actual beans with incised designs in graves, regards the markings as ideographic writing, but, if they are, nothing is known of their meaning. In some cases messengers are shown with wings and wearing humming-bird masks; in fact masks of various types as well as face paint are common.

Fig. 8

Prisoners are shown naked, generally with a rope round the neck, but class distinctions are maintained even here and they were made to carry their captive chiefs in litters, stripped like themselves of everything except in some cases their head-dresses. Sometimes they were executed by being thrown down a precipice, and since a tusked god is often the executioner, this was probably a sacrifice to the god. Very frequent is a more or

Plate 23

less human figure, with feline tusks to represent a god, who is probably the successor of the feline god of Chavín times, and he appears so often and in so many guises that he must have had a dominant place, though he no longer held the monopoly.

Plate 22

Fig. 8. Two Mochica warriors fighting. Painting from a vase. Both hold maces with pointed staves. The victor, who has knocked off his opponent's helmet, holds him by the hair. He wears shirt and helmet decorated with a design like a medieval 'gyronny' coat of arms. The device on the left is a trophy of arms, which includes two maces, two darts and a square shield. Humming-birds hover above. (Redrawn from Larco.)

There are other gods in the form of fish, bats, birds and other animals with partly human forms or merely human limbs, also completely grotesque demons which may emerge from great conch shells.

Warriors carry small square or round shields and maces with

Plate 24 *Fig. 8*

Fig. 8

pear-shaped heads, sometimes flanged, with the staff pointed at the other end to serve as a spear, and when fighting they grasp the hair of an opponent in the moment of victory. They may fight with a copper axe, with convex blade, held in the hand. Copper-tipped lances and spear-throwers are found in the graves, and both may have been used in war, but the spear-thrower is more often depicted in hunting scenes on the pottery. Weapons are sometimes shown alone on pots, in which case they may be personified by being given some human features, and the remains of a polychrome fresco on one of the great pyramids at Moche appear to represent them in revolt against their human masters. Music and dancing have their place on some vases. Panpipes are very frequently represented, and are played by gods, men, or even skeletons in a sort of dance of death. There are actual pottery trumpets, both straight and looped, and conch shells with the end removed were used for the same purpose, as indeed they still are on the Peruvian and Ecuadorian coasts. Pottery whistles were in use, particularly the spherical ones built into whistling jars, and so were notched flutes of bone and pottery, of a type still used in Peru under the name of quena, and actual examples are common in addition to representations on pots. Rattles were made of pottery, metal or strings of large seeds, and, again, they are depicted on pots, as are drums and tambourines.

Human beings suffering from various diseases are vividly shown on some of the pots, and others appear to have been deliberately mutilated by the amputation of limbs, lips or nose, perhaps as a punishment. There are some few vases, which have the form of a potato with painted or modelled 'eyes', sur-mounted by a human head with the mouth mutilated to resemble the eye of the potato, and it has been suggested that this was a form of magic to stimulate the fertility of the plant. Amputations may have been done also for medical reasons, and circumcision was practised. There are representations of medicine men performing cures by sucking the affected part to remove a foreign body, which is still a well-known shamanistic practice. Ghastly figures, naked and with the face flayed, are depicted tied to a frame and exposed to birds of prey, and it is believed that this was the mode of execution of persons guilty of serious crimes. Some modelled vessels show scenes of sexual activity, and it is noteworthy that most, if not all, are perversions of some sort, in contrast with the natural ones on the earlier Salinar vessels. They are far from common and form but a small proportion of the very large collections of Mochica pottery which exist, so when it is considered that a vessel of this kind is bound to attract attention it is clear that they do not necessarily indicate that these practices were particularly prevalent. Larco states that they are confined to the latest stages of the Mochica Culture.

Representations on pottery are not confined to the supernatural, the spectacular and the abnormal, and almost anything may be shown. There is even an instance of a man washing his hair! The animal and vegetable worlds are well shown. There are deer, fish, foxes, frogs, monkeys, snakes and other animals, but birds in particular are beautifully modelled or painted, and the species can sometimes be identified. Owls are particular favourites, and human figures with owl faces, wings and tails are often found. The naturalistic jaguar shown attacking a prisoner on Plate 23 is a rare type. Among vegetables there are maize, potatoes, squash and gourds. Gourds were also sometimes used as containers, and they may be decorated with incised designs.

Plate 25

The Mochica buried their dead lying on the back in an extended position in a rectangular grave, which may be lined with courses of stones, or with rectangular adobes in which niches are contrived for the reception of offerings. The bodies are often wrapped in cloth, which is rarely well preserved, and sometimes enclosed in bundles of canes or in cane coffins, or in rare instances they may be protected by large jars or parts of them. A piece of metal wrapped in cloth, gold, silver or copper according to the degree of the dead, was commonly placed in the mouth, and instances occur of cane tubes extending to the surface of the ground, which Larco interprets as vehicles for offerings of food or drink, although they could possibly be for the passage of the spirit.

A striking instance of the burials in canes was excavated by Professor Strong at the Huaca de la Cruz in the Virú Valley. In a rectangular pit about 11 feet deep, which appeared to have been hastily dug, he found the remains of a man wrapped in fine cotton cloth inside a bundle of canes with a copper plate in his mouth, accompanied by several Mochica jars. On removing this, a rectangular cane coffin with the remains of a coarse covering of twill was seen, and with it were two headless sacrificed llamas. The crouched remains of two sacrificed women were found outside the coffin at two opposite corners. The coffin was opened and inside was a rich array of grave goods, including 27 jars of late Mochica type, gourd bowls, three boxes made of wooden slats wrapped with coloured thread, and the decayed remains of feather fans and ornaments and elaborate head-dresses. In their midst were three wooden staves, which were old when buried and had been repaired. One was a war club with a pear-shaped head carved with an elaborate fighting scene, and a socketed copper point. The second had a carved owl sitting on the top, and the third was a copper-shod ceremonial digging-stick on the top of which was carved the figure of a god in human form with feline tusks, wearing a loin-cloth and a semi-circular head-dress with a feline face in front and a cushion-like protuberance at the back. The staring red and yellow eyes, the tusks and other features were marked by shell inlay, some of which was missing. At the god's right hand stood a small boy with a large mouth, which may formerly have had feline tusks, holding some lumps

See *Bibliography*, Strong and Evans, 1952

Fig. 9

of turquoise. There can be no doubt that the pair were meant to represent the feline god and an attendant, in the character of the patron of agriculture, and that the turquoise grains were maize which the boy would plant while the god dug, just as the women still plant the seed while their husbands dig with the taccla or digging-stick.

When most of these things had been removed, the skeleton of a small boy was found on the left side of the coffin. He had

Fig. 9. Tusked god and boy from the head of a ceremonial digging-stick in the burial of a Mochica Warrior-Priest, Huaca de la Cruz, Virú Valley. Height about 6 in. (Redrawn from Strong.)

a deformed skull and a heavy jaw, he was wrapped in cloth and some gilt copper plates were sewn to it round his waist. Beneath him was a horizontal cane partition which occupied most of the coffin, and under this was the body of an old, old man wrapped in cloth, with the remains of a head-dress like that on the god on the staff, a gilt copper mask inlaid with turquoise over his mouth and a simple copper mask over his face. He and the boy clearly represented the two figures on the digging-stick, but the war club and the owl staff show that the old man had other functions as well, and Strong has justly called him the Warrior-Priest. The significance of the owl staff is not known, but it doubtless betokened some kind of authority, and the whole assemblage indicates the dual character, religious and secular, of the Mochica rulers. Why was he buried hastily with his venerable insignia? The pottery belongs to the very last stages of the Mochica Culture, when the art was showing signs of weariness and disintegration, and the Mochica domination was soon to be eclipsed by the arrival of invaders bringing new ideas from the south. It may be that the death of the old man brought a dynasty to an end, and perhaps the enemy was already at the gate.

NORTH
HIGHLANDS

In the northern highlands, there are two very different aspects of the culture of the Classic Period, neither of them known in great detail. The more northerly, in the Cajamarca Basin, was entirely independent of outside influences from any Peruvian area yet studied, between the modified Chavín Period already mentioned and the end of the Classic. During this time there arose a pottery style known as Cursive, from its lightly painted

Plate 29

running designs which vaguely recall writing, in brownish-black, sometimes also in red, on a white or cream ground. Highly stylized animals or animal heads are sometimes included in the painting. Most of the vessels are open bowls of various forms on ring bases. Large plain cooking pots on tall tripod feet appear here in the Classic Period, a feature which suggests very strongly that there were contacts with the Ecuadorian Andes, although there is no sign of the Cursive style there.

Plates 26-8

In the Callejón de Huaylas is the remarkable pottery style of Recuay. This consists of vessels decorated with black negative designs over white and red, one of the most characteristic being a highly stylized feline in profile with an elongated comb projecting from the head. There is a great deal of lively modelling different in character from the Mochica and inferior to it. A

very typical feature is a broad, nearly horizontal flange sur‚
rounding the mouth of a jar. Highly stylized and rather crude
stone statues representing warriors and women are linked to
Recuay by some of the incised designs which adorn them, and
it is believed that some rather elaborate stone buildings of two‚
or three storeys, roofed with stone slabs, may belong to it.
Recuay graves are stone‚lined, and may be a simple box or a
gallery. In general, this area demonstrates the highland prefer‚
ence for stone over adobe as a building material, which is a

*Fig. 10. Two bowls, painted in black, white and red. Inter‚
locking style, Classic Period, Central Coast. Approximate
height 7 in. (After Kroeber.)*

reflection not only of its availability but of the wet climate with
its regular rains.

The central coast is an area of minor importance in the CENTRAL COAST
Classic Period, and it has not yet been possible to learn much
about the nature of the buildings or the distribution of the
population. A polychrome pottery style called the Interlocking
links a number of valleys, and gets its name from the small,
angular interlocking units, some apparently purely geometrical Fig. 10
and some derived from animals and fish, or their heads, which
may cover the surface after the manner of some of the textiles.

F

The interlocking designs may occupy a limited area such as a border, or be replaced by scattered ones of the same character. It is known that the important ceremonial site of Pachacámac, a short distance south of Lima, was occupied at this period, and most of the ruins in the lower Rimac Valley, in which Lima lies, appear to belong to it. Among these is a notable group of rectangular adobe pyramids variously called Aramburú and Maranga, where Professor Kroeber excavated a number of extended burials, mostly wrapped in cloth and lashed to a litter made of canes, generally face downwards and accompanied by a single pot or nothing at all.

SOUTH COAST
Nazca Culture

In the south coast, the Classic Period is represented by the Nazca Culture. Until the recent work of Strong, this was chiefly known from the polychrome funerary pottery, which is extensively represented in museums all over the world. Practically nothing was known about any dwellings or ceremonial centres. Strong's work is very recent and only a brief summary is available, but he found what he describes as a great capital at Cahuachi in the Nazca Basin, though it is not clear whether it can properly be described as an urban centre. It includes wattle and daub rooms, walls built of conical adobes, platforms and pyramids.

The Nazca Culture was confined to three comparatively small valleys, those of Nazca, Pisco and Ica, and it differs from the Mochica in not providing any evidence for expansion or aggressive tendencies. In view of the smaller area and smaller population, the irrigation canals did not need to be on such a large scale, and no fortifications have been discovered. The pottery does not provide the same sort of evidence about the structure of society as that of the Mochica, but, such as it is, it indicates an interest rather in the supernatural than in the rank and occupations of men. The burial tradition of the south continued, and huddled, cloth-wrapped mummies were buried in circular chambers, approached from the surface by a shaft. The textiles were not as rich or abundant as those of Paracas, but their production doubtless absorbed a great deal of the time and energy of many workers, to a degree which the grave offerings of the north coast, which consisted predominantly of mould-made pottery, could not have done.

The pottery was thin, well fired, and, in contrast with the Mochica, was painted in many colours. The ware is buff or red, and it is painted in up to eight colours, the most usual being shades of red, yellow, brown, grey and violet, together with black and white, the designs being outlined with black in some cases. Several chronological stages were distinguished on typological grounds by Kroeber many years ago, the chief being an early one, Nazca A, and a late one, Nazca B, with a mainly post-Classic Nazca Y. Strong's stratigraphical work has confirmed this, but he has added an early stage before Nazca A, of which details are not yet available. Most Nazca A pots have rather a sombre red background to the designs, and white backgrounds are usual in B. Bowls and beakers of various types are the commonest forms, but double spout and head and spout jars are very characteristic. Modelling plays a very minor part and seldom goes beyond the head on a jar; the one man band belongs to Nazca Y, when modelling is more frequent. The painted designs fall into two main groups, the first consisting of recognizable but stylized life forms, such as birds, fish or fruits, and the second of religious and mythological themes, such as complex demons; for example, a centipede with a feline face, which may wear a mouth-mask like the metal ones that are found on some mummies. Some of these demons carry human heads, which are also a very common feature by themselves, generally forming part of the painted decoration on a vessel but sometimes a whole pot. The frequency of this motif shows that the head cult, to which attention has already been drawn, was very strong at this time. The treatment of the human face in Nazca art is highly characteristic and is not confined to the pottery. There is a strong likeness between the

Plate 30

Plate 31

Plate 32

Plate 34

Nazca pottery demons and those on the Paracas Necropolis textiles, which implies that there cannot be any very great difference in age between them.

When the traveller by air looks down on the desolate pampas round Nazca, he sees a multitude of long, straight lines, geo-

Plate 35

metrical figures and other markings on the ground, a pheno-menon which has not been observed elsewhere in Peru except on a small scale in the Virú Valley. They were formed by removing the dark brown crust, rich in iron oxide, which covers the yellow sandy surface in this neighbourhood, and piling it up round the exposed areas. The lines may radiate from a point in almost any direction, form parallel groups, or be distributed irregularly, and they vary from half a kilometre to more than 8 kilometres in length. They are associated with elongated, solid areas of more or less rectangular, trapezoidal or triangular form, one of the largest being 1700 metres long with a mean width of 50 metres. Spirals and zigzag lines are frequent, and there are irregular forms besides occasional birds and fish. Lines frequently intersect and figures may be superimposed on one another, but examples of the various types are associated in a way which suggests that no great time difference is involved. Their actual age is a mystery, but a clue is that some animal forms have appendages which recall in a vague way those of some monsters on Nazca Y or even possibly Nazca B pots. Their object has not been satisfactorily explained; the best sug-gestion so far is that the lines were for making astronomical observations for calendrical purposes, and that the elongated geometrical figures were the result of adjusting a line as the position of the first appearance of a star above the horizon varied over a period of years. This does not explain the zigzag lines and curvilinear forms. Whatever the explanation, the setting out and execution of these perfectly straight lines and other figures must have required a great deal of skill and not a little disciplined labour.

The remaining area where cultures ascribed to the Classic Period are known is the southern highlands, with its two important sites at Tiahuanaco and Pucara. Of these, Tia⁄huanaco is by far the better known, and in view of its wide⁄spread influence on subsequent developments, its importance is very great. The ruins, with their imposing stonework, attracted attention long ago, and not only have they suffered greatly from the plundering of the stones for building, but they have been the victims of a great deal of unsound speculation, which has ascribed an absurdly great age to them on ridiculous grounds. Tiahuanaco is believed to have been a ceremonial centre under strong religious control, and it was perhaps built with the aid of pilgrims, as has been suggested for some of the Formative sites. The art is stiff, formal and impersonal. The neighbourhood lies at a great height and is cold and bleak, but it supports a fairly large scattered population and may have done so in the past. It is suitable for the herding of llamas and alpacas, and the growing of potatoes and grains like quinoa. The ruins consist of a number of units, each of regular construction, but their relation to one another is haphazard. There is a stone⁄faced stepped pyramid, more or less triangular in plan, made by improving a natural hillock, and on the top are foundations of buildings and a reservoir. Near by is a rectangular enclosure measuring 130 metres by 135 metres, formerly slightly raised, with the remains of a dressed stone retaining wall consisting of upright stones alternating with a filling of smaller rectangular blocks, most of which have disappeared. Within it, at one end, is a smaller enclosure, approached from the outside by a wide stairway of six great monolithic steps between a pair of massive uprights, which form part of the wall common to the outer and inner enclosures at that end.

Some stone statues have been found in these enclosures, and a most striking feature, standing in one corner of the outer enclosure, is a great monolithic gateway, cut from a block of   Plate 36

85

Fig. 11

lava 12 feet 6 inches by 10 feet, bearing a central carved figure at the top, dominating a frieze of three rows of attendants, below which is a border of frets enclosing faces like that of the central figure and ending in condor heads. The central figure stands facing the front and holding a staff vertically in either hand. The hands lack the little finger. The staves have condor heads at the lower end, and that in the right hand, which is probably a spear-thrower, has a condor at the upper end to represent the hook, while that in the left hand is bifurcated and terminates in two condor heads at the top. It may be intended to represent a quiver containing two darts. The trapezoidal head of the figure is surrounded by a halo of appendages, which include six puma heads on long necks, each with a ring balanced on the end of the snout like a lump of sugar, and the face has round, staring eyes from which fall bands bearing circles, suggesting tears. Condor and puma heads are repeated on the body of the figure, and from his belt hangs a row of faces, perhaps trophy heads. He is generally said, without any certain evidence, to represent a great creator god of Peruvian mythology, who in much later times was recorded by the Spanish chroniclers under various names, the best known being Viracocha. The attendants, who run in towards him, have faces like his own, but in profile, or condor faces, and are dressed in winged cloaks bearing numerous condor head appendages. They carry staves similar to his. The weeping eyes, the running figures, and above all the condor and the puma, represented so differently from the felines of northern Peru, are features which recur constantly wherever the influence of Tiahuanaco is felt.

There are other units, of which the chief are a rectangular enclosure, and a platform or pyramid, much destroyed, which was built of very large stone blocks, some of which weigh over 100 tons. Associated with this are many remarkable carved blocks, including some with recessed geometrical decorations, such as squares with stepped sides, and some very large ones

containing niches and doorways, which may have been parts
of chambers with monolithic walls. The stones composing
this and other Tiahuanaco masonry may be fitted and held in

*Fig. 11. Central figure from monolithic gateway at Tiahuanaco.
Height about 2 ft. (After Joyce.)*

place by means of accurately cut notches or by copper cramps,
straight or T-shaped at either end, set in grooves.

A number of massive monolithic statues have been found in
and around Tiahuanaco, the largest being 24 feet in total

height. They resemble pillars bearing relief designs rather than true sculptures in the round; clothing is indicated by lightly incised designs, and the figures may carry beakers or unidentified objects. Other carvings include slabs with relief designs, and heads tenoned for insertion into walls. It is natural to suppose that the incised designs on the statues are derived from textile patterns, but the same may probably be said of the carvings on the monolithic gateway, and although no highland Tiahuanaco textiles have been preserved, very similar designs appear on coastal ones which were subject to Tiahuanaco influence. Classic Tiahuanaco pottery lacks some designs found on the stonework, such as the full-face standing figure, which appear on coastal pottery and textiles, and there is no stonework on the coast, so it is most likely that textiles were the main vehicle for the passage of Tiahuanaco designs from highlands to coast.

The only stratigraphical excavation at Tiahuanaco was done by Bennett in 1932, and he was permitted to work only on a very limited scale. He established a succession of periods marked by pottery styles, comprising a Classic which is believed to correspond to the major building works, preceded by an Early Period, and succeeded by a Decadent one. The typical decorated Classic pottery is a fine, polished polychrome, which most commonly has a red slip and designs painted in yellow, grey or brown, black and white, or some of these colours. The colours, originally bright, may weather rather faint and indistinct. Pumas and condors in profile, with eyes divided vertically into black and white halves, are common designs, and so are geometrical figures such as steps, triangles and the combination expressively called the step fret. Like all Tiahuanaco art, the designs are stiff and formal. The shapes include a tall, graceful, hollow-sided beaker, the kero, and various types of bottle and flaring-sided bowl, including modelled puma vessels. The Early Tiahuanaco polychrome vessels are decorated in

Fig. 12
Plates 39, 42

shiny black, white, red, orange and brown, direct on the micaceous buff clay or on a slip of the same colour. There are characteristic interlocking geometrical designs, and curious animal forms, with divided eyes, which look more like broken-down, stylized developments than primitive ones, although they are quite different from the Decadent Tiahuanaco designs. A very typical Early Tiahuanaco shape, the 'spittoon', is illustrated in Plate 38. The post-Classic Decadent stage shows greater frequency of geometrical designs, the breakdown of animal forms, with repetition of eyes or heads instead of whole figures, and a general degeneration in execution. Colours become duller, and lack the polish of the Classic Period. Among vessel shapes, the beaker or kero becomes less graceful and may have a disproportionately small base. Decadent Tiahuanaco may have continued in the home area in Bolivia for a long period, until shortly before the Inca Conquest in the fifteenth century.

Fig. 12. 'Kero' or beaker. Classic Tiahuanaco. (To show the form, not the decoration.) Height about 6 in.

The Classic Tiahuanaco Culture in its pure form has a limited distribution, although a few sites with its masonry, its pottery or both have been found in the neighbourhood of the type site. The area has not been very fully explored, but it is most unlikely that any centres of the period comparable in importance with Tiahuanaco have escaped notice. On the other hand, clear signs of Tiahuanaco influence in the shape of characteristic designs without some features of the total culture, for example the stonework, are widespread. Derived Tiahuanaco, as Bennett calls it, in one form or another, is found in the Eastern Cordillera in Bolivia, at Huari in the central highlands, and in many parts of the coast, but its developments in the two latter areas belong to the next chapter.

Pucara lies some distance north-west of Lake Titicaca on the side opposite to Tiahuanaco, near a station on the Juliaca to Cuzco railway. This is well known to travellers as a flourishing pottery-making centre at the present time, and well-made

Pucara

89

bulls and other objects are laid out for sale beside the line. The excavations there have not been fully described, but it is known that the site includes rough, probably domestic, buildings of undressed stone, and a well-built sanctuary. This consists, at ground level, of a series of horse-shoe-shaped walls of red sandstone, made up of straight sectors, which enclose a slightly sunk terrace bounded by white sandstone slabs, and containing a sunk court, some fifty feet square and seven feet below the terrace, also bounded by tall white sandstone slabs and entered by a stair. The outer horse-shoe wall includes in its thickness a series of small chambers, entered from the inner side, each containing one or two altar-like slabs. The central court has a stone-lined grave chamber containing several burials, in the centre of each side. The original height of the walls is unknown, and there is no evidence that the structure as a whole was roofed. There are surface indications that there were other similar structures on the site. The masonry is not so well fitted as that of Tiahuanaco, and chinks may be filled with adobe or pieces of stone.

Apart from the walls, the stonework consists chiefly of statues and standing slabs or stelae. The statues are mostly rather less pillar-like than those of Tiahuanaco, and generally represent a man wearing nothing but a breech clout with curious square side flaps and some form of cap. He may hold a trophy head and possibly a knife. The stelae frequently have a step cut out of one side at the top, and are carved with fine champlevé or incised designs which generally take the form of a lizard-like creature with a ring above the head, or of complex geometrical figures, mostly made up of elements like checkers, stepped crosses, jagged zigzags, diamonds and chevrons, suggestive of textile patterns.

Among a variety of plain red and brown mica-tempered pottery wares is a highly characteristic polychrome. This is made of a reddish-buff micaceous paste very similar to that used in Early Tiahuanaco, and designs are either painted direct in red and black on the natural colour, or in black and rather fugitive yellow over a red slip. A highly characteristic feature is that the outlines of the colour patches are incised. No whole vessels have been found, so our knowledge of designs and shapes is imperfect, but there are puma or cat figures in profile with the head shown full face in low relief, human and condor heads in profile, concentric circles in black and red, and geo-metrical figures such as stepped lines. Eyes are divided vertically like those of Tiahuanaco animals, but the natural buff of the clay may take the place of the white. Another feature which the two cultures have in common is the ring balanced on the nose of a cat. As far as can be deduced from sherds, the commonest forms are a flat-bottomed bowl with flaring sides, and a bowl with a low ring base.

Plate 37

Pucara pottery and sculpture have demonstrated the distri-bution of the culture over the area between the type site and the north-west end of the Lake, but it has not been found else-where. Its relation to Tiahuanaco is uncertain, they have features in common but there are many differences. No chrono-logical stages have been distinguished, but on the whole it gives the impression of being rather older than Classic Tia-huanaco.

CHAPTER VI

The Expansionist Period

THE CLASSIC PERIOD was succeeded by the Expan-sionist Period, the first stage of the post-Classic, which has been given this name owing to the wide and rapid spread of features associated with Tiahuanaco. It has been conjectured that the stage was set for this expansion by the development of a general state of unrest, the chief outward expression of which was the Mochica conquest of the valleys to the south of their original home. Elsewhere, the isolation of the north highland culture of Cajamarca began to be broken down, and there are signs that the influence of Recuay was making itself felt on the coast.

The appearance of Tiahuanaco elements on the coast was sudden and catastrophic. The chief signs of the change are the introduction of a new art style in most of the coast and part of the highlands, and the appearance of new types of settlement and southern burial customs in the north coast. Although there is clear evidence for the influence of Tiahuanaco in all this, it is not a simple case of an invasion of the coast by Tiahuanaco people. There are features in common between the two areas but many differences—there is a Bolivian Tiahuanaco tradition and a distinct Peruvian one. Peruvian Tiahuanaco has many varia-tions, which emerge more strongly as local traditions in the coast make themselves felt, but, at the beginning, the style which is called Coast Tiahuanaco A indicates a considerable degree of unity over the whole area, and it is expressed chiefly in the pottery and textiles over the whole coast from Nazca to Moche.

The stone carving and building which is so characteristic of Bolivian Tiahuanaco is altogether absent from the coast. Several features which belong to it and which curiously enough do not occur on Bolivian Tiahuanaco pottery, are constantly found on the coastal pottery and textiles, where they are associated with divided eyes and other features shared by highland pottery. Among these Classic stone-carved designs are the full-face standing figure from the great gateway, its face alone, and the running winged figures which accompany it; details may be modified or simplified, for instance, puma heads may replace condor ones in some positions, and the 'tears' on the face of the central figure may be elaborated into trophy heads or simplified into wavy lines, but it is clear that it is intended to show the same personages. It has already been suggested that these designs may have been transferred to the coast from the highlands largely by means of textiles, but this may not be the complete explanation because the colour scheme of the pottery in both areas is similar, whereas that of the textiles, preserved only in the coast, is always somewhat different and may be totally distinct. Both highland and coastal pottery are well made and polished, the ground is generally red and the designs are painted in black, white, yellow and grey though the colours normally remain more vivid on the coastal pots. Although many of the shapes in the two areas differ, there are two in common, the beaker or kero, and a cup of squatter proportions, but there is a tendency for the sides to be straight instead of concave on the coastal examples. Some textiles have a red ground, with designs worked in yellow, white, brown and blue, and in these cases the scheme is not very unlike that of the pottery, since blue has taken the place of grey and brown that of black, but in a large group most of the area is occupied by yellows and oranges or light browns, with details in a number of colours, including blue, green, red, pink, black and white. Too much must not be made of the differences, since we do not know enough about the exact chronology, or the availability of different dyes, to be able to assess the importance of these factors.

Plate 41

Some consideration may now be given to the general result

of these changes, and to the way in which they came about. In the south coast, highland designs began to appear on vessels of Nazca shapes in the late stage which has been called Nazca Y. The next step was the obliteration of the Nazca Culture, which never reappeared, and the same applies to the Interlocking pottery style of the central coast. In the north, in the valleys of Virú, Moche and Chicama, the Mochica Culture was sub, merged or driven out, but its relative strength is shown by the fact that elements of it, particularly the modelling tradition in pottery, reappeared later, when local cultures developed again, although much was changed.

Huari

See *Bibliography*,
Bennett, 1953

There is an intermediate site between Tiahuanaco and the coast, which has made the relations between them somewhat clearer, namely, Huari (or Wari) in the Mantaro Basin in the central highlands, which was the subject of Bennett's last work. This was a great habitation site with a good deal of rough walling. It also contains some stone statues and a little dressed stonework of a ceremonial nature, in the form of subterranean chambers on one, two or three levels, which may be a link with the stonework of Tiahuanaco, although it is less elaborate and lacks copper bonding cramps. The pottery includes a poly, chrome which is in the coastal or Peruvian tradition, with such features as the standing figure with his staves, skulls, rows of chevrons, profile puma and condor heads but not whole animals, and so on. There are other, non-Tiahuanaco, pottery styles at Huari, which Bennett regards as representing a local development, although some types may show influence from Nazca, and others, such as a local cursive style, are almost certainly due to influences from the north, since there are also some cursive sherds in distinctively Cajamarca style, which must have been carried from there.

A great deal remains to be done in the Mantaro Basin, and the predecessors of the Huari Culture have yet to be found and its own distribution traced, but Bennett considers that the best

explanation of the facts as we know them is that the introduction of the distinctively Tiahuanaco designs on pottery, and
perhaps the stonework, was due to an invasion of an established
culture by alien elements from Tiahuanaco. He shows reason to
believe that the Huari Culture at the type site was rather later in
date than Classic Tiahuanaco. The total Huari Culture was
not carried on to the coast, any more than the total Tiahuanaco
Culture was carried to Huari; it was the religious symbols
which travelled, the standing figure with his attendants, the
trophy heads which he carries, and the cat and condor heads
with which he is adorned, and they seem to have been carried
on mortuary textiles and to a lesser extent on ceremonial pottery
in a form which had developed at Huari. The conclusion is
inescapable that the expansion was basically religious in
character, but its catastrophic effects show that it must have
been backed by military force.

More can now be said about the special features of Coast
Tiahuanaco. Apart from the Virú Valley, most of our knowledge is derived from grave goods in cemeteries and we have
little information about the buildings. At Pacheco, in the
Nazca Valley, is a cemetery that is known for its polychrome
pottery, which takes three rather special forms. There are large,
thick, U-shaped urns with flattened bases, decorated with some
of the best coastal examples of the full-face standing figure,
which may have been made to contain mummy bundles.
There are also fragments of large, boldly painted human heads,
and large vessels in the form of a llama, with a collar-opening
set in the back.

In the central coast, the best-known cemeteries are at Ancón
and Pachacámac, and these contain many mummy bundles
with finely woven wrappings, buried in conical or cylindrical
chambers, with a covering of wood, stone, cane or mats. The
best and most usual of the textiles at this period are of tapestry,
but all the older techniques continued in use. Two processes,

SOUTH AND
CENTRAL
COAST

Plate 33

which if known before had rarely been used, now became common, namely, knotted pile cloth, used chiefly for making square caps, and a method of tie dyeing in which pieces of the cloth are gathered up and whipped round with waxed thread before dipping, to resist the dye, leaving rows of diamond, shaped outlines in the colour of the undyed cloth. By an in, genious application of this method, a patchwork of squares of different colours, bearing contrasting diamonds, was built up, and large pieces were sometimes used to wrap mummies.

The ikat method of tie dyeing is believed to have been intro, duced towards the end of the period. This process, in which the warps are dyed before weaving, the pattern being produced by wrapping those portions which are not to be dyed with waxed thread before dipping, is fairly common in modern times in western South America. It was extremely rare in Ancient Peru. Only four examples have been reported, belong, ing either to this period or the subsequent one, from the north and central coast. The rare occurrence of such a highly special, ized technique suggests introduction from outside Peru, and it is tempting to look to Indonesia, but, until something is known of its age there, speculation will be profitless.

Tapestry designs include not only close copies of the Tia, huanaco figures already mentioned, but also various degrees of

Plate 41

stylization, of which the most extreme are abstractions in which little can be recognized except the divided eyes. Apart from the beakers and cups which have already been mentioned, highly characteristic Central Coast A forms are the double, spout, and, bridge jar, with rather long, tapering spouts, and jars with a modelled face on the collar. As time went on, the Tiahuanaco symbolism began to break down, and rather an ill, defined Coastal Tiahuanaco B stage was reached. Signs of this are seen in what Uhle long ago called the Epigonal style, which may still retain recognizable Tiahuanaco characteristics like the

Plate 43

divided eyes on the head cup from Huacho, though in general

the designs show evident signs of degeneration, with a tendency to break up into geometrical patterns. The stylized tapestries mentioned above are evidently a product of the same trend. The full development of Coastal Tiahuanaco B is reached in the black-white-red pottery style with purely geometrical decoration. In company with the painted pottery styles of later Coastal Tiahuanaco stages are found red and black wares with pressed relief decoration, prominent among which is coarse stippling, which may form the background to human or animal figures or scrolls.

Plate 54

Besides pottery and textiles, many objects of various kinds have been found in Coast Tiahuanaco graves, and they show that wood, shell, metals, bone and stone were worked with equal skill. Among the most interesting are the carved wooden paddles and centre boards with which rafts like the Kon-Tiki were steered. The examples illustrated are from Ica, in the south, and their ornamental carving shows that they were probably made for burial in the graves in which they were found, but plain ones exist. Those illustrated may possibly belong to the subsequent period, but Coast Tiahuanaco examples exist, and they show that coastwise travel on rafts was already possible at this time, although it was never the main means of communication.

Plate 50

In the north, the Virú Valley survey has told us what little we know about the effect of what may be called the Tiahuanaco-Huari crusade on mundane things such as domestic pottery and buildings, as well as on the temples and forts. To deal with the latter first, both the large pyramids and the Gallinazo-Mochica strong points went out of use, and the main type of structure which can be regarded as a public building is a large high-walled rectangular compound without interior divisions, of which three examples were found in the lower part of the valley. The walls were of adobe, in the massive cast form known as tapia, and some of them survive to a height of ten

NORTH COAST

G

See *Bibliography*,
Willey, 1953

feet. Their function is uncertain, but the discoverer, Professor Willey, considers that they may be some sort of religious or political meeting place. Groups of dwellings or small villages, enclosed within more or less rectangular compound walls of smaller size than the previous type, also came into vogue. A typical example of medium size measures 60 feet by 40 feet. The walls have foundations of stone in the upper part of the valley, and of tapia in the lower part, surmounted in each case by plain rectangular adobe bricks. The interior is divided into rooms, with courts and corridors, and in some cases there is a low pyramid or platform, perhaps a kind of domestic shrine. The introduction of this type of dwelling did not mean that the older ones all went out of use; a considerable number of the unenclosed clusters of houses were still in-habited, and it is only natural that much of the original population should continue to live in their old homes. The introduction of the enclosed type of village is believed to mark the beginning of the trend towards the urbanization which was characteristic of the following period, and outside Virú there

Plates 51-3

is evidence that Chan-Chan, near Trujillo, the greatest urban site of the Chimú in later times, was already occupied, though nothing is known of the scale of the occupation.

There is little published evidence about the burials of this period in the north, but from a statement that graves were a yard or less in diameter in the Virú cemetery we may infer that the custom of burying the dead sitting in a crouched position was introduced from the south at this time. This has recently been confirmed by Collier's work. Cloth-wrapped mummies of this form were common in the north in the subsequent City Builder Period.

See *Bibliography*,
Collier, 1955

The pottery in Virú showed marked changes with the fall of the Mochica. Grey and black wares became predominant on the domestic sites, showing the mastery of the reducing flame in firing, and the old distinction between domestic and funerary wares became less marked, so that decorated pottery is found in some quantity in the household rubbish and plain wares are occasionally found in graves. The black and grey decorated forms are extremely varied in form, and include such types as double vessels, double-spout-and-bridge jars, and canteen-shaped bottles. Their decoration is in pressed relief, and takes the form of geometrical designs such as angular step-frets or curvilinear scrolls. Some have slightly sunken areas bearing pictorial designs such as men holding staves, moons, or cats, in low relief against a stippled background. These wares are closely related to those already mentioned from the central coast. Plain black or grey jars with an applied face on the collar are also common. In earlier times, the changes in domestic wares from period to period were so gradual as to suggest that they developed locally, but at this time there is a strong indica-tion of the import of wares of a different tradition from outside. The source of these black and grey wares is believed to be the far north of the coast, the Lambayeque and neighbouring valleys, and it has been suggested that their arrival in Virú may be due to a forcible removal of part of the population by the highland invaders, a foretaste of Inca practice. The obvious difficulty about this very interesting suggestion is that there is little evidence of Tiahuanaco-Huari intrusion north of the Chicama Valley. Further study of the far north is needed to clarify the matter.

It is not possible to say exactly where the relatively pure Coast Tiahuanaco A stage and the decadent B stage fall in the Virú Tiahuanacoid sequence, since the characteristic painted pottery types are funerary and are insufficiently represented on the living sites which have been studied; but the typical A polychrome and the black-white-red geometrical B ware are both present. The B stage is also represented by a special type of face-collar jar with pressed relief pictorial designs on the body, painted in subdued black, white and red over a buff ground. The two stages are similarly represented in the valleys of Moche and Chicama.

Plate 44

The Tiahuanaco expansion in the north did not stop short on the coast, but affected the north highland basin of the Calle/ jón de Huaylas also. Its influence here is shown in a painted pottery style which is closely related to Coast Tiahuanaco A of the central and south coasts, found associated with local wares including a negative black/on/red or /orange, and others appar/ ently related to the north coast. This assemblage was excavated by Bennett in domestic rubbish as well as in stone/lined graves, some of them eight feet deep. Other Tiahuanaco/influenced wares are found in local collections, but their associations are uncertain.

The effect of the Tiahuanaco contact does not seem to have been very profound, since the pottery is associated with a great deal of stone building, which is rather rough but which in a general way continues the local tradition of Chavín and Recuay. Besides the tombs, there are houses built of rough stone, with one or two floors, containing from one to four rooms, roofed with stone slabs with earth piled on the top. There are also a few examples of a more elaborate type of building of similar construction, which Bennett has called temples. He has described one of these called Wilkawain, with three storeys each containing seven rooms with ventilating shafts, which is built of split but undressed stone, laid in alternate rows of thick and thin stones, with the interstices chinked with small stones. The alternation in thickness provides a faint reminiscence of the fine masonry of Chavín. The temple has a projecting course of stones at the top, with a recessed one beneath it, and below this was a row of cat heads tenoned in, but all of them have now been lost. This work has nothing in common with the stone masonry of Classic Tiahuanaco, and it is clear that the Tiahuanaco influences reached this area by way of the coast and not along the highlands.

Farther north, in the highland area to the east of the Chicama Valley, are a number of sites of the Expansionist Period, which are altogether free from Tiahuanaco influence. Chief among these is the great fortified hilltop of Marca Huamachuco, con, taining many buildings whose walls survive to a considerable height, grouped about a circular citadel and enclosed within a great outer wall. The walls are skilfully built of irregular stones, a type of masonry which is called pirca in Peru, and some buildings had two or even three storeys. It may be that these fortifications were a reaction, which proved successful, to the menace of the Tiahuanaco-Huari expansion. Ornamental stone-carving is found here, and it includes stylized feline heads with zigzag crests and tenons for insertion into walls, besides small slabs carved with step frets. Among the pottery, some types seem to be local, and there is a cursive style which seems to be derived from Cajamarca, which is not far away, but what stage in the Cajamarca succession it belongs to is not known.

In the Cajamarca Basin itself, the influence of the expansion was felt, and pottery of various Tiahuanacoid styles has been found there. The Reichlens, who have studied the region, have claimed that these include not only coastal types, but also Huari and Decadent Tiahuanaco sherds from the highlands. If this is so, they must have by-passed part of the intervening area, including the Callejón de Huaylas, in their travels, but this is quite possible, since pure Cajamarca cursive-style sherds were found, it will be remembered, at Huari. The Tiahuanaco influence made itself felt gradually, and was not strong enough to oust all the local characteristics, since cursive designs at first continued in use on a reduced scale, subsequently giving place to felines and heads of felines painted in a cursive manner, after which these in their turn broke up into symbolic designs. All this decoration was painted in black and red or black and orange on the local white or cream paste, on small tripod and ringed-based bowls, which were local forms.

Cajamarca in its turn influenced the coast. Open bowls on ring bases or tripod feet, decorated in pure cursive style, are

Cajamarca

See *Bibliography*, Reichlen, 1949

found occasionally in the coastal valleys between the Lam- bayeque region and Moche, in Coast Tiahuanaco contexts, but they are almost certainly trade pieces from the type area. Later on, probably through their agency, appeared a coastal style called Cursive Modelled, which is believed to belong to the earliest stage of the Chimú Culture of the subsequent City Builder Period. It belongs in the same northern region but its range extends south to the Santa Valley. It is found on spout- and-bridge whistling jars, which are surmounted in most cases by modelled figures, and have long, tapering spouts. The ware is buff or reddish buff, and the typical painted decoration con- sists of red stripes, between which are black patterns such as zigzag lines, running scrolls, and scale patterns. It is the manner of execution of these rather than the patterns themselves which suggest derivation from the Cursive style.

CUZCO   The evidence for the sudden beginning and gradual fading of the great expansion in the various areas of the Central Andes has now been reviewed, but a conspicuous gap remains. No mention has been made of the Cuzco region, and in spite of its proximity to Tiahuanaco no conspicuous remains of the period have been identified there, although a Tiahuanacoid pottery horizon has recently been identified, followed by local pre-Inca styles. It was suggested at one time that the early Incas were already settled at Cuzco and were able to resist outside pressure, but this is ruled out by the new discoveries.

The most recent estimates of the duration of the Expansionist Period do not allow it more than 300 years, and place its beginning at about A.D. 1000; no radiocarbon dates for the period have been determined, but if any reliance can be placed on those available for the Classic Period, it probably began several centuries earlier.

CHAPTER VII

The City Builder Period

THE EXPANSIONIST PERIOD was brought to an end by the emergence of three states on the coast, one of which, the Chimú in the north, was large and powerful enough to be described as an empire. In all three, great urban centres were built, whence the name City Builder, which has been applied to the period of independence of these states, before they fell to the conquering Incas. It has already been suggested that the idea of the planned centre of population, within a compound wall, was brought from the south in the Expansionist Period, since structures of this kind on a small scale were already in use in Virú at that time. Huari itself is unlikely to have been the source of the idea, since the plan of the greater part of that site is not sufficiently regular and most of the surviving walls do not appear to belong to houses. Perhaps the origin is to be sought in the south coast, where Strong has found what he calls, in his preliminary account, a city of the Classic Period at Cahuachi in the Nazca Valley. The building of the cities and the con/ centration of large numbers of people there is an index of the nature of the period, which was one of social and political development with little technological advance. The people had been organized in Classic times, but the process was intensified now, and the city plans, where they have been studied, appear to have been developed with a view to imposing strict control.

Two types of urban site have been distinguished in the Chimú area, and we may for convenience describe them as cities and towns. Both include rectangular units, containing planned groups of dwellings enclosed in massive walls, but some at least of those in the cities are more elaborate, and contain in addition terraced buildings with large rooms. These have walls richly decorated with textile/like designs modelled in

Plate 51

Plates 52, 53

relief in mud plaster, as well as courts and mounds, and are believed to have been the dwellings of the ruling class and the cult centres. The towns seem to have served two purposes. Some are built in strategic positions, particularly at the places where valleys open out from the foothills on to the coastal plains, since it is here that the main irrigation canals are taken off; these would have accommodated garrisons. The others are situated in large irrigated areas, and would have been the homes of the labourers who worked them.

Although there were no notable advances in techniques at this time, with the possible exception of the invention or at any rate the limited spread of bronze, there are changes of emphasis, and in pottery and textiles there are signs of a tendency to mass-production. In metalwork the casting of copper was employed on a larger scale than before in the production of ornaments, useful objects like the blades of digging-sticks, or weapons such as mace-heads. Gold, silver, copper and their alloys were used abundantly in making vessels and articles of personal adorn-ment and use, such as crowns, ear ornaments, collars, armlets, lime spoons and thin sheet ornaments for sewing to garments. In pottery there was a tendency to standardization and reduc-tion in the number of colours. The modelling tradition revived in the north, but it was dull and lifeless by comparison with that of Mochica times. Elsewhere, entirely new styles evolved. Textiles are similar over the whole coast, and to distinguish between those of the different areas is a specialized task. Cloths of many types, predominantly of cotton, were made in abun-dance, but perhaps the most characteristic are garments adorned with regular rows, horizontal or diagonal, of conventionalized birds, animals or fish. These are generally brocaded, or worked in double cloth, in which case the field may be divided into squares of two alternating colours, each charged with a device of the opposite colour. Tapestry is normally confined to borders and other small areas, and embroidery is limited similarly.

Plate 47

Plate 45

Plates 46, 49

Feather-work is frequently found, feathers of various colours being sewn to a cotton cloth to build up a design, such as the stylized owls on the poncho figured in Plate 57. Feather head-dresses are often associated with such garments, and in the example illustrated a rectangular flap bearing owls like those on the poncho hangs down behind.

The best examples of textiles and feather-work, together with baskets, decorated gourds, and objects of wood, bone, shell and other materials, come from the graves. Throughout the coast, the normal form of burial is the mummy bundle, in which the crouched body is wrapped in textiles and the bundle provided with a false face usually of wood or metal, although pottery masks may be used. Neither at this nor at any other time was any process of embalming employed; the entrails were some-times removed and the cavity stuffed with grass, but this was by no means the rule and, in general, preservation is due entirely to the dry climate. Most bodies are quite dried up, but the slowness of decomposition in some cases is illustrated by a Chimú mummy found by Strong in Virú, which emitted such a foul smell that it was most unpleasant to work around, in spite of the lapse of at least 500 years. The grave goods differ greatly in elaboration according to the status of the deceased, and the graves themselves vary from a simple pit marked at the surface by an upright stick or paddle, to a square chamber roofed with canes or mats supported on beams, sometimes con-taining two mummies accompanied by pots, weaving instru-ments, beads and other grave goods.

In the Virú Valley, there was a great reduction in the number of sites, and most of the surviving ones were in the neighbour-hood of the shore. It may be that they depended for cultivation chiefly on plots of ground called pukíos, excavated down to the water table, which can only be reached in that way near the coast, and that the irrigation canals which had served most of the valley were in decay. Both of the main types of settlement,

NORTH COAST
See *Bibliography*,
Willey, 1953

the enclosed compounds and the irregular clusters of rooms, were still present, but the trend towards the first type continued. The population of the valley had clearly been drastically re, duced, and very likely large numbers of people had been moved away, perhaps to Chan-Chan in the Moche Valley to the north. Virú had become a backwater and no great town or city was built or occupied there, although those rectangular compounds which contain mounds are like the characteristic city enclosures in miniature, and one has been found with some remains of mud plaster relief decoration on the entrance jambs.

Chimu

The date of foundation of the Chimú kingdom in the Moche Valley is uncertain, but the latest estimate is by John Rowe, based on post-Conquest writings, which puts it in the first half of the fourteenth century, though it can hardly be as late as this if the radiocarbon dating of the earlier periods can be relied on. Like the Mochica in the same region, it spread over the adjacent valleys, Virú being an early victim, and by the time it fell in its turn to the Incas in the middle of the fifteenth century, the Chimú dominion stretched from Tumbez in the far north nearly to Lima. It was a despotic state, and Rowe suggests that the Incas learnt many of the characteristic features of their civilization from it, including the rectangular city plan and mass production of goods.

Plates 51-3

The Chimú capital was Chan-Chan, and this is the out, standing example of the type of city referred to above. It covers an area of about eleven square miles, and contains ten or more large, walled, rectangular enclosures, oriented more or less in one direction but not in direct relation to one another. Each of these could have been the dwelling, or at least the headquarters, of some such division of the nation as a clan. In the spaces between them, there are irrigated areas, reservoirs and ceme, teries, and on the outskirts is a great irrigated area with small compounds, and stone buildings which appear to guard canals and roads, as well as large cemeteries. There are also numerous sunken pukíos, now full of reeds.

The enclosures average about 1300 feet by 650 feet, but some are larger, and the walls, which may be double or triple, stand up to a height of as much as 40 feet in places. The most usual building materials are rectangular adobe bricks, set in mud mortar, and often disguised by a coat of mud plaster, which makes them look like tapia, the puddled variety of adobe. The latter is used also, and so is a sort of clay concrete, mixed with stone and shell. The compounds vary in plan, but most of them contain a palace-like building with its decorated walls, inner compounds containing small rooms, perhaps for retainers, a stone-lined reservoir, irrigated plots, a pyramid, generally of modest dimensions, and rows of cells, sometimes described as prisons but which could equally well have been storerooms. The walls have no parapets, no means of access to the tops, and few entrances, and they seem to have been disciplinary rather than defensive.

The development of great cities of this type is believed to have been dependent on the combination of the irrigation schemes of more than one valley, and in the case of Chan-Chan water was derived from Chicama as well as Moche. The towns which were built to defend and work this system illustrate both the types mentioned above. One of defensive character is in the narrow part of the Moche Valley, up which it straggles for five miles, occupying terraced hillsides and small side valleys, and it includes regular compounds of both stone and adobe. It commands three of the main canals. The other, which consists mainly of scattered compounds, lies in Chicama in the midst of an area, formerly irrigated, alongside the great canal which led to Chan-Chan. Examples of all three types of settlement are found in the valleys farther north, and the diversion of water from one valley to another is illustrated by the existence of two great cities in small valleys adjacent to the large one of Lambayeque, from which water had to be taken in order to support them. The many buildings and the irrigation systems must have required a great deal of organized labour for their construction and maintenance, but an even greater problem must have been posed by the constant supply of food to cities like Chan-Chan. There was of course no wheeled transport, and although llamas were used they can carry very little even in their own mountain home, so the bulk of the food must have been carried on men's backs. As far as is known, there was no medium of exchange, so the distribution of food must have been a function of authority.

Although the roads of Ancient Peru are generally thought of in connection with the Incas and spoken of as Inca roads, inter-valley roads were always necessary to the coast states, and quite vital to the Chimú Empire, with its great extent along the coast. The Incas made use of them also, but they were more concerned with communications along the highlands, and between the highlands and the coast, so the principal coastal roads must date from pre-Inca times; the Incas may have modi-fied them in some sections. It is even possible that the Chimú had something to teach the Incas in this matter as in others. There are almost continuous traces of a road from the Motupe Valley just north of Lambayeque to the Chao Valley just south of Virú, with remains even farther south in Santa, Nepeña and Casma, which ran the greater part of the length of the Chimú Empire and must have existed at the time of its greatest extent. The remains differ in elaboration, and like our own roads they tend to be wider and more imposing near the great centres of population. In the deserts between valleys they were tracks between very low walls, or even marked by posts only, but in valleys the simplest type is a levelled surface 15 to 25 feet wide, enclosed between walls of stone or adobe about 3 feet high, though one of this type widens out to 80 feet as it approaches Chan-Chan. In some places the surface of the road is raised, and it may be flanked by canals. Some have an outer pair of walls 80 to 160 feet away from the road, enclosing cultivated fields.

Not much in the way of frontier defences has been observed in the Chimú area, which may be partly due to insufficient search, but it is probable that any work of this kind was con-centrated on places where a threat was believed to exist. Much of the area was of course bounded on the east by uninhabited, barren hills. Paramonga, in the Fortaleza Valley, is a great terraced structure built of rectangular adobes, which is believed to be a fortress. It crowns a spur overlooking the valley, which is near the southern limit of the Chimú Empire, and it may have served to overawe a recently conquered people.

Plate 56

The Chimú Culture is familiar to many through its pottery, which is abundant in many museums. The most usual type is polished black ware, and the commonest shape is the stirrup-spouted jar, revived from former times in a somewhat modified form, with the spout generally squared in section and a small modelled animal or projection applied where the arch joins the upright. Other common types are the jar with a spout con-nected to a modelled figure by a flat bridge, and the double whistling jar with modelled figures standing on it, both of which are of southern origin; both may have been made in this sort of ware before the end of the previous period, but they are much more frequent in Chimú times. Decoration is chiefly by modelling in the round, normally in moulds, application, and pressed relief, the llama head illustrated being of better quality than the general run of modelled figures, which are far inferior to most Mochica work. Similar work is done in polished red ware, but it is not nearly so common, although a good deal of undecorated domestic red ware has been found at Chan-Chan. Painting is rare, but occasional modelled vessels decorated in black or black and red on a reddish-buff ground are found, including the cursive modelled type already described.

Plate 55

Plate 58

South of the Chimú was a much smaller state, which occupied the Chancay, Ancón and Rimac valleys in the central coast. The chroniclers give it the name of Cuismancu. Urban centres are found in this area also, and the chief of these is Cajamarquilla in the Rimac Valley above Lima; no plan of it has been published but it probably belonged to the city type. As in other parts of the coast, adobe was the main building material, but there was a greater use of tapia here than in the north. The chief archaeological evidence for this state is the existence of a single late pottery style in these valleys. The ware is thin, dull red or cream in colour, with a creamy white slip, decorated with textile patterns in black. The chief shapes are an egg-shaped jar with a flaring collar and a pair of small loop handles, a similar jar with a modelled human face on the collar and skimpy limbs in low relief, and bowls of various types which may have a ring base. Both form and decoration are derived from the local expression of the black-white-red style of late Expansionist times, and the dropping of the red colour, as well as the poverty of the modelling, gives an impression of degeneracy.

Plate 59

cf. Plate 54

On the south coast was another state, the Chincha, which occupied the valleys of Chincha, Pisco, Ica and Nazca, to which may perhaps be added Cañete, at its northern margin, on the strength of the presence of the Ica pottery style. The chroniclers describe Chincha as a powerful state, which made incursions eastwards into and beyond the mountains, and they say that it was only conquered by the Incas after fierce battles, but the archaeological evidence does not suggest that it was organized to the same degree as the Chimú. There are some imposing ruins in the Chincha and Ica valleys, but true urban sites are rare. The ruins are much damaged, but although the plans are generally rectilinear in character, most of them give the impression of being grouped about a ceremonial nucleus, with terraces and pyramids. There are rooms and courts, but

they are believed to be either ceremonial or the houses of important people, and do not point to large concentrations of
population. This may be a reflection of the smaller size of the
valleys of the south. Tapia is a common building material, but
hard rectangular adobes are also used, and they are so much
better in quality than modern ones that Dr. Uhle observed that
they fetched ten times as much when sold for building houses,
a fact which has resulted in much destruction.

The Ica pottery style, which provides the archaeological
evidence for a political unit in this area, is found in all the
valleys enumerated above. It grew out of the Tiahuanacoid
Epigonal style, and passed smoothly through various stages,
which differ only in minor details; after a time, Inca features
appeared on some of the local forms, and then Inca influence
increased until the arrival of actual Cuzco types, which apparently marked the subjugation of the state by the Incas. The
vessels are made of hard, well-burnished, buff or dull red
ware, covered with painted decoration in black, white and red, Plates 60-1
in the form of textile-derived patterns, which are chiefly geometrical but include small birds and fish. The commonest
forms are globular or ovoid jars with constricted necks and
flaring collars, and bowls with angular outlines and solid,
chamfered rims. Other bowls have a gently convex base which
meets the sides at a sharp angle; the sides slope slightly inwards
and may be shallow and almost straight, or deep and concave.
A variant of this form, with a blunt junction at the base and
a more pronounced outward curve at the top, is shown in
Plate 60.

The highland basins, with their broken topography and HIGHLANDS
multiple sources of water supply, are not so suitable for large
concentrations of population as the flat coastal valleys, and
urban sites of this period have not been recognized within the
highland basins. There are developments east of the Cajamarca
Basin, in the Valley of the Marañon in the Department of

Amazonas, which will for convenience be mentioned here, although their age has not been determined. Full publication of these is not available, but M. Reichlen has reported that he has discovered great walled towns near a place called Kuélape. These have mummies built into the walls. In the same neigh, bourhood are mummies with an outer casing and a false head made of stone and mud plaster, set up in groups on ledges on cliffs. There are also curious little gabled stone houses up to three storeys in height, built against cliffs in fairly inaccessible positions, to contain burials. They are painted red and white, and have ornamental T-shaped niches or openings in the out, side walls. All the burials found had been disturbed, so their original form is unknown.

It is not known whether these three types are contemporary or not, but all suggest a comparatively late date. The large towns may belong to this period, but they may also be related to the fortified site of Marca Huamachuco, belonging to the Expansionist Period. The mummy bundle type of burial belongs to one of these two periods elsewhere in the north, and the local variety with an outer casing may be an adaptation to the wetter conditions of the Marañon Valley. The nearest parallel to the three-storey burial houses is in the stone temples like Wilkawain, in the Callejón de Huaylas, also belonging to the Expansionist Period. It is probable that all these develop, ments would have reached this remote spot later than their appearance in the main centres of civilization, so they are probably of the City Builder Period. No Inca influence has been reported.

In the south highlands, the Tiahuanaco Culture passed through a period of decadence of unknown duration, of which the tangible evidence is the Decadent Tiahuanaco pottery style. It is believed to have ended before Inca influence reached the area in the fifteenth century. After its disappearance, a large number of stone burial towers called chullpas were built in the

Plate 62

area. They may be round or square, built of fine, dressed masonry or rough stones. Most have the burial chamber inside them, but some of the rough ones are solid, and the chamber is then excavated in the ground beneath them. It is not certain to what extent the differences are due to chronology, but the solid type with an underground chamber is believed to antedate Inca influence in the area, and the others to be later than its arrival. The final Inca conquest of the district took place about 1470, but they fought there earlier and their influence may have been felt as early as 1430. The chullpas are associated with various pottery styles, chief of which are either plain, or black on red. One of the latter types has been found stratified between Classic Pucara and Inca remains at Pucara, which serves to confirm its relative age. No decadent Pucara, corresponding with Deca-dent Tiahuanaco, has been found, and it is probable that the site and its sphere of influence were eclipsed in their prime by Tiahuanaco itself.

While these developments were taking place in the high plains round Lake Titicaca, and the coastal states were build-ing their cities, there was still nothing very spectacular in the Cuzco Valley. There was rather a lowly early Inca culture there, and the evidence for it will be described in the next chapter.

CHAPTER VIII

The Imperialist Period

THE INCA EMPIRE, after which this period is named, spread from small beginnings to its utmost limits in about 90 years, and in so doing it overflowed the limits of the Peru, vian area to cover much of Ecuador in the north and Chile in the south. It was a true empire, a term which cannot properly be applied to any other ancient American state except the Chimú, but it must still be emphasized that the features which went to make up the Inca Culture and Empire were the result of the gradual growth of Peruvian civilization, which we have traced from its beginnings, and not of the import of anything from outside.

The name Inca is used in various ways, as will be seen later, but in its origin it belonged to a group of tribes which were living in the neighbourhood of Cuzco before the fifteenth century, and spoke the Quechua language. Inca pottery and other material remains are greatly different from any of those which preceded them at Cuzco, showing that they must have come there from elsewhere. This is supported by the legend, which has been published many times, concerning their origin, the substance of which is that four brothers and four sisters, with their followers, emerged from caves some eighteen miles south, east of Cuzco, and started on a leisurely journey in search of good farm-lands, where they could settle. They carried a golden staff with which they tested the depth of soil. Three of the brothers were disposed of in various ways, and eventually the remaining one, Manco Capac, with his three sisters, chose the site of Cuzco, and after expelling the inhabitants, founded the city there. Although the story is legendary, the first Inca ruler of Cuzco whose name is known with any degree of reliability was called Manco Capac.

The place where the Inca actually came from is not known, but there is no reason to suppose that they travelled very far, and their origin is most likely to have been in the same highland zone where they settled down, and not, as one theory has claimed, in the coast, since in this region of great contrasts in height people are at their best at the altitude in which they have always lived. Various versions of their list of rulers were recorded by the chroniclers of the sixteenth and seventeenth centuries, and Rowe has sifted these and reached the conclusion that a list of thirteen names, beginning with Manco Capac and ending with Huayna Capac and his two sons Huascar and Atahuallpa, can be relied on. Using this list he has estimated that the Inca dynasty at Cuzco began about 1200.

During the course of his archaeological excavations there Rowe has found remains of the Early Inca Period, which is defined as the time between their first settlement and the beginning of their great conquests in the fifteenth century. He has discovered wall foundations of rough stone, burials, and accumulations of domestic rubbish. The cooking pottery consists of buff ware, some of it very rough, and there are painted wares with a buff paste, decorated in black, or black and red, either directly or over a white slip. Designs are entirely geometrical, and not unlike those on late Inca wares, but are not so finely executed. The shapes also are generally similar to the later ones. It is not a very remarkable series of wares, and its importance lies in the fact that it is clearly ancestral to the typical late Inca ones. Little metal has been found, but there were ground slate knives and bone tools. Burials were of the seated, flexed type, wrapped in cloth or mats, like the mummy bundles of the coast, and they owe their preservation to their position in beehive-shaped stone tombs built in cracks in the cliffs, which kept them dry.

Like most Peruvian highland Indians, the Inca were rather short and stocky, averaging about 5 ft 3 in. in height, with broad shoulders, and the deep chests associated with a people who live in the rarefied atmosphere of the high Andes. They had a brown skin, straight hair, rather a broad face with a prominent nose, straight or slightly hooked, and little facial hair. The coastal peoples were very similar in appearance, but generally rather slighter in build.

For the first two centuries after their settlement in Cuzco, the Inca seem to have been involved from time to time in plunder, ing raids and minor wars with neighbouring tribes, but there were no permanent conquests. Other tribes were similarly engaged, and by the beginning of the fifteenth century the more prominent among them were the Lupaca and the Colla in the Titicaca Basin, the Quechua who adjoined the Inca on the north-west and the Chanca beyond them. The Quechua pro, bably shared a common language with the Inca and were friendly with them. The Lupaca and the Colla were at enmity with one another, and Viracocha, the eighth in the line of Inca rulers, allied himself with the Lupaca; this probably marked the beginning of Inca influence in the Titicaca region. Meanwhile the Chanca defeated the Quechua, and prepared to attack the Inca when Viracocha was old and feeble. He and his son and heir designate, Urcon, left Cuzco for a more defensible spot, but another son, afterwards the Emperor Pachacuti, refused to leave and led a desperate resistance. The Chanca were repulsed and afterwards soundly beaten, leaving the Inca in a position of power. Pachacuti was crowned, in 1438 it is believed, and the great Inca conquests began.

Unlike the previous wars in the district, the Inca campaigns were not mere raids, and the conquests were consolidated and made permanent. Being a highland people, the Inca naturally made their first conquests in their own environment, and Pachacuti spread his empire over the highlands from near Lake Titicaca in the south-east to Lake Junin in the north-west, by about 1460. His son Topa Inca, a man of equal ability, was by then old enough to be associated with him, and together they greatly enlarged and consolidated the Empire. Topa Inca fought his way north to near Quito, whence he invaded the central part of the Ecuadorian coast near Manta, where there was a sanctuary of some renown. From there he is said to have made a voyage to some islands on a raft made of balsa logs, a craft particularly characteristic of Ecuador to this day, since the tree grows there in abundance. The story may well refer to an island called La Plata, which can be seen from the neighbourhood of Manta, since Inca remains have been found there, or with less likelihood to the Galápagos Islands where Peruvian coastal potsherds, probably from the Chimú area and culture, have been found. After this, Topa Inca attacked the Chimú Empire from the north, the direction whence trouble was least expected, and subdued it without serious difficulty, continuing southwards to Pachacámac.

Although some tribes, like the Cañari of Ecuador, put up a bitter resistance to the Inca, their conquests did not always involve fighting, and diplomacy, in the shape of a combination of threats and promises, backed by the approach of an organized army, often sufficed to bring about the submission of an enemy. Of the Chimú, Professor Willey writes: '. . .the great valley irrigation systems were highly specialized means of sustaining life, and because of this specialization they were vulnerable to attack and disruption. With the urbantype life of the later periods, the dense population centers imprisoned in narrow valley oases would have appeared as overripe plums to the more mobile highlanders.' When the Chimú had submitted, it seems that they were allowed to go on living much as they did before; in fact, recent writers have suggested that Chimú Culture influenced the Inca much more than the Inca affected the Chimú, so that many features of the later Inca Empire were derived from the coastal state. Even after its absorption in the Inca Empire, the Chimú black ware pottery style, blended with

See *Bibliography*, Willey, 1953

Inca forms, continued to spread southwards on the coast, and it is found in increasing quantities in Inca times in the southern valleys of Chincha and Ica. As Kroeber said many years ago, neither the native Cuzco nor the native Chimú ware spread at all widely; but a blend of the two, with a heavy proportion of black ware, flooded Peru shortly before Pizarro.

While Topa Inca was engaged on these campaigns, Pachacuti concerned himself mainly with the organization of the Empire, and the rebuilding of Cuzco and the shrines and buildings in the neighbourhood, until he resigned his Empire to his son in his old age in or about 1471. At about the same time, Topa Inca undertook a new expedition against the south coast of Peru, and after he became Emperor he invaded the lowlands to the east of Cuzco, but soon had to turn back and suppress a rebellion of the Aymara tribes in the Titicaca region, led by the Colla and Lupaca, now allies. He then pushed on and conquered highland Bolivia and north-west Argentina, after which he descended into Chile, where he fixed the southern boundary of the Empire on the Maule River, about 35 degrees south latitude.

Topa Inca died about 1493 and was succeeded by Huayna Capac his son, the last undisputed ruler of the Empire. He spent much of his time in administration and in quelling minor revolts, but also conquered the Ecuadorian highlands north of Quito after a bitter struggle, on the shores of a lake still called in the Quechua tongue Yaguar-cocha, the Lake of Blood. He extended his dominion in the coastal plain of Ecuador also, and conquered the island of Puná in the Gulf of Guayaquil, but parts of the coast between there and Manta were never subdued. When he died of a pestilence in 1527, he had heard of the arrival at Tumbez of the first Spanish expedition. The remainder of the story is well known—the succession of Huascar as Emperor and the successful revolt of his half-brother Atahuallpa, who was seized by Pizarro and his handful of followers in the moment of victory.

Wherever the Inca spread, there is tangible evidence of their presence. Many of their buildings have disappeared, but examples are still found at widely separated points. A constant feature is the trapezoidal opening, doorway, niche or window, and buildings containing them are generally made of adobe on the coast and stone in the highlands. Coastal examples which may be mentioned are the 'palace' at La Centinela in the Chincha Valley, where there may also have been a temple, and the great 'sun temple', with its attendant buildings, which was put up to overshadow the ancient sanctuary at Pachacámac. In the hills, Inca ruins are found at least as far north as Ingapirca in the Province of Cañar in southern Ecuador.

Plates 1, 71

In its homeland round Cuzco, Inca masonry takes several forms, and at one time it was believed that they indicated differences of age, but it is now known that all date from the great period in the fifteenth century. The differences are primarily ones of function. There are two main types, one composed of polygonal blocks, generally of large size, and the other of regular courses of rather small rectangular blocks with sunk joints. The polygonal type is used chiefly for massive enclosure walls, and for the main retaining walls of terraces, and the best example, the three ramparts of the great fortress of Saccsaihuaman, which dominates Cuzco, contain stones up to twenty feet in height. The rectangular type is generally used for buildings, and the finest of all, which is flat, without the sunk joints, is derived from it and is used for special buildings. An example of the latter is the famous curved wall, which lay beneath the sanctuary wall of the Dominican church in Cuzco until the earthquake of 1950 relieved it of that load, and another seen on the right of Plate 1, belongs to what must have been an important shrine in the remote city of Machu Picchu. A modification of the polygonal type of masonry is built of much smaller polygonal stones, and is sometimes described as cellular; it also is used both in buildings and in terraces. More

Plate 70

Plate 69

than one type may be seen in a single wall, for instance, rectangular masonry may be used for convenience on either side of
a doorway in an otherwise cellular wall. This fine stone walling,
of whatever type, was used mainly for public buildings, such

Plate 69

as the palaces of the Incas, temples and the houses of the Chosen
Women, generally called the Virgins of the Sun. The average
dwelling was probably of irregular field stones set in mud, of
turves set in courses, or of adobe, and Rowe has suggested that
the polygonal masonry was an elaboration of the irregular
stone-walling, while the rectangular type with sunk joints was
inspired by the turf construction.

In all the fine masonry, the stones fit perfectly together at the
surface of the wall, in spite of the fact that the softest stone used
in the Cuzco district is comparable in hardness with the Car-
boniferous Limestone of Yorkshire, and a good deal of it is of
igneous rocks which are much harder. They are believed to
have been worked roughly into shape with stone mauls, and
finally ground in with blocks of sandstone, but whatever the
method, the story that not even a knife blade can be inserted
between them is no exaggeration. Many of the stones must have
been brought from considerable distances, and the very
impressive remains which are incorporated in the Spanish
buildings of Cuzco, or stand deserted elsewhere in the same
district, bear witness to the abundance of regimented labour
which the Incas had at their disposal. The buildings depend
for their effect on their massiveness and fine finish, and the
exteriors have little in the way of ornament, although it is
known that the thatched roofs were finely worked into patterns.
Even the trapezoidal niches are mostly found inside the buildings, and representational carving on buildings is extremely
rare, since there are practically no examples beyond a few very
small snakes and pumas on some buildings in Cuzco.

On the other hand, portable objects may be carved with
some elaboration. Flat-bottomed stone dishes are highly

characteristic Inca objects, and many of them bear snakes on the outer wall or have lugs in the form of animals instead of handles. The example figured is exceptional in its elaborate low relief figure carving, but it is of particular interest by reason of the woman spinning with a falling spindle as she walks, just as modern highland women do throughout the Central Andes. It is possible but unlikely that this dish is just post- Conquest, and this way of spinning was almost certainly in use in the highlands by Inca times, although the lighter spindle, supported in a bowl, was always popular on the coast. The carving on this dish is stiff and rather crude, but some examples of another type of object are real works of art, namely, small stone figures of alpacas with a cylindrical hole in the back which are found buried in the fields. Crude pottery models of alpacas are still used for fertility ceremonies near Cuzco and are subsequently buried in the yards where the animals are kept, so it is inferred that the stone ones were used for the same purpose.

Plate 64

Plate 63

In its homeland around Cuzco, Inca pottery is of excellent quality, and is made of a few standard wares in a few standard shapes. Cooking pots, namely, a pedestalled bowl with a broad loop handle and a cover, and two forms of tripod, one a bowl and the other a peculiar vessel opening at the side, were made of hard plain brown ware, but it is the painted wares that are most characteristic. These are highly polished, and are nor- mally polychrome, the usual colours being red, white, black and yellow, but orange may be found also, particularly in a provincial variety made near Lake Titicaca. There are a number of varieties, but they can be grouped together under the generic name of Cuzco Polychrome. Some attractive vessels are decorated with rows or a scatter of little painted stylized animals, birds or insects, but these are not the most common, and the usual designs are geometrical, for example, diamonds, checkers, parallel stripes, cross-hatching and saltires.

There is also a very frequent design like the backbone of a fish, consisting of a central rib and a row of parallel lines, each ending in a knob, on either side, which may be a conventionalized plant.

Of the shapes, the most typical is the jar to which the name of aryballus has been given, with a conical base and tall, flaring neck. In origin it was a large jar for carrying water and perhaps chicha, a maize beer which is still largely used in the Andes, and it was designed to be carried on the back, with the aid of a rope which passed through the two vertical strap handles and over the nubbin below the neck; the nubbin is generally modelled in the shape of an animal head. A great many were made in smaller sizes, down to miniatures a mere six inches high. Another very typical form is a shallow saucer, with a handle in the form of a bird's head or less usually a loop on one side, and a pair of minute projections opposite to it. Jugs and bottles with flat-strap handles are common also, and so are straight-sided keros or beakers, a form which was also made in wood and decorated with inlaid scenes and figures in coloured lacquer. Wherever the writ of the Incas ran, these forms are found, but they were made, generally in a modified form, of the local wares. Thus it is quite common to find a short-necked aryballus, with no nubbin, made in the Chimú black ware and decorated with pressed relief. In Chile, both aryballus and saucer were made in local polychrome. Local shapes were also modified by the introduction of Inca details; for instance, a tall neck with flaring mouth, derived from the aryballus, is often found on double whistling jars in the Chimú region, and the form persisted into post-Conquest times, because examples with a European green glaze are sometimes found. Reference has already been made to the wide distribution of a blended Chimú-Inca style.

In the use of metals, the chief innovation associated with the Inca was the spread of bronze throughout the Empire, even

Plate 67

Plate 65

Plate 66

to such remote parts as Ecuador. Tools and weapons were cast in both copper and bronze, and forms particularly associated with the Inca are a flat, trapezoidal axe-blade with ears to assist in binding it to the haft, and the tumi or knife, with handle projecting at right angles to the blade. These metals were also used for making decorative and ceremonial objects, such as pins and figurines. They were the only metals available to commoners, gold and silver being reserved to the Emperor, to privileged nobles, and to the use of religion. Most of the surviving objects are of thin sheet metal, hammered into shape, but accounts given by the chroniclers suggest that they were sometimes made solid. Characteristically Inca objects of these metals are little figurines representing men, women, llamas and alpacas.

Plate 48

The Empire expanded, as has been shown, with great rapidity, and as it grew its organization was built up. The Emperor at its head was an absolute monarch, and in the great period he was a son, though not necessarily the eldest son, of his predecessor. Although the name Inca is often applied to his office without qualification, he was properly called Sapa Inca, meaning Unique Inca, and he had other titles, including Intip Cori, Son of the Sun, in reference to his supposed direct descent from the sun, by virtue of which he was worshipped as a god during his lifetime, as well as after death. His despotism was a benevolent one, and he cared for the material welfare of his people, because he knew that this was necessary for the prosperity of the State and his own well-being. He had a chief wife, the Qoya, who from the time of Topa Inca was his full sister, but he had many secondary wives also, by whom he had many children.

The male descendants of each Emperor formed what was called a royal ayllu, and these formed the original aristocracy, the Incas by blood. The word ayllu denotes the groups into which most Andean tribes were divided; the ayllu appears to have been a kin group, an enlarged family or group of families, with descent in the male line, and marriages took place within the group. It has sometimes been called a clan, but it was not one in the strict sense, since clans have descent in the female line and marry outside the group. The Inca made use of the ayllus of conquered tribes, but regrouped them if necessary to make village units of convenient though variable size, so that they sometimes became groups of unrelated families. Each ayllu held lands which were divided into three portions, one for the Emperor, one for the Sun, and one for the ayllu itself; the cultivation of the first two was the normal form of taxation, and the products were used for the maintenance of government and religion. The ayllus were grouped into provinces, and within each province the ayllus were classified in two, or in large provinces three, moieties, analagous to the Upper or Hanan, and the Lower or Horin, divisions of the original Inca tribes. The provinces in their turn were grouped in the famous four quarters of the Empire, Chinchasuyo in the north-west, Cuntisuyu in the south-west, Antisuyu in the north-east, and Collasuyu, including the Titicaca area, in the south-east, which met in Cuzco along lines running approximately north and south, and east and west.

The administration of these and smaller divisions required a multitude of officials, and by the time of the Spanish Conquest a twofold noble class had been evolved, the Incas who held the higher posts, and the Curacas, who were less important. The original Incas by blood, the royal ayllus, numerous though their members had become, were insufficient to fill all the higher posts, and Pachacuti created a new class of Incas by privilege, derived from other Quechua-speaking tribes. All were distinguished by special headbands and large ear-plugs, whence the name Orejones, or Big-ears, given them by the Spaniards. The curacas included some of the chiefs of conquered tribes who had submitted without opposition, and they had charge of administrative units of a hundred taxpayers and upwards. Both classes were hereditary and exempt from taxation.

The four quarters and the provinces were ruled by Inca nobles, and within the provinces the ayllus were grouped and divided into units of approximately 10,000, 5000, 1000, 500 and 100 taxpayers or heads of families, each under its curaca of appropriate grade. Under them were non-hereditary officials in charge of 50 and 10 taxpayers. The people were further divided into twelve age groups, each with its defined duties and exemptions. It has been stated already that the normal form of taxation was agricultural work, but there was also a special labour levy, the mit'a, for the army, the roads and other public works, and the mines. Specialists of various kinds paid their tribute in the employment of their skills or abilities; thus, there were the runners who were posted along the roads to carry messages by relay, the metal-workers and the tapestry-weavers. Specialists were supported out of public stores, but those who were away from home temporarily on the mit'a tasks had their lands tilled and their families supported by their ayllu. So efficient was the system that it is said that the Incas called out the mit'a to perform unnecessary tasks in order to keep the people from idleness and mischief.

Women were not free from organization and control. An Inca official visited the villages at regular intervals to inspect any girls who had reached an age of about ten. He divided them into two classes; those of special beauty or promise were sent away to be educated in special institutions by the State, or reserved for sacrifice on special occasions or in emergencies, such as the accession or serious illness of an Emperor, and the remainder were left behind, to be married in due course to the boys of the village by the curaca, who picked their mates for them. Those who were taken away were placed in convents called Accla Huasi, the Houses of the Chosen Women, in the

Plate 69

provincial capitals or in Cuzco, and here they learnt such things as spinning, weaving, and cooking. Those destined for sacrifice were regarded as fortunate, since they were assured of a life of ease and comfort in the world to come. The others were divided into those who would be given as wives to nobles or successful warriors by grace of the Emperor, and the Mamaconas, some of whom would be secondary wives or servants to the Emperor, and some dedicated in perpetual chastity to the service of the temples and shrines. Those who served the Emperor included specially skilled weavers, who made fine clothing for him.

Fig. 13

The numbering of the people and their produce required a special class of accountant, the quipucamayoc, who were skilled in recording the figures on the quipu, an arrangement of knotted strings of various thicknesses and colours, on which different numbers were recorded with knots of various sizes. It is unlikely that they could have been used for recording anything except numbers, and records of a particular commodity—quantities of maize or chicha for example—were probably decipherable by different quipucamayoc from those who could read the census records. The same accountants are now believed to have used an abacus, and in both it is likely that a decimal system was employed, unlike the arithmetic of the Maya, which was vigesimal. A form of quipu is still used by Andean herdsmen to keep count of their flocks, but the surviving ancient examples are from coastal graves. Most of these are believed to date from the Inca Period, but the idea may be as old as the Mochica since quipulike objects are painted on some of their pots. There is no record of any system of weights among the Inca or other Peruvian peoples, and the way in which quantities were measured is uncertain. Small balances with beams of the order of six inches long, made of richly carved bone or wood, or of metal, belonging to various periods, are found on the coast, but they can only have been used for very small

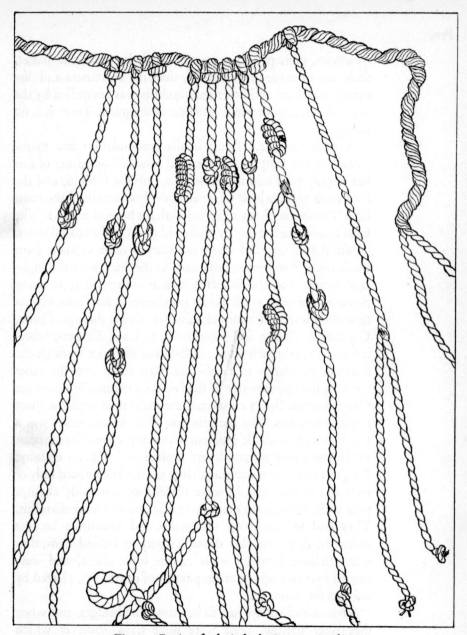

Fig. 13. Portion of a 'quipu', the Inca counting device.

quantities, perhaps of precious material. Beyond local barter, there was no trade in Inca times, since the movement and distribution of food and other commodities was controlled by the State, and transport was a function of the mit'a. There was no money.

A most important factor in the consolidation and maintenance of the Empire was the road system. Something of this has already been said in connection with the Chimú, and the Inca coast road, which traversed the whole length of the coast from Tumbez to Arequipa, and perhaps beyond it into Chile, must have consisted largely of the old roads of the coastal states, modified and extended where necessary in order to make them continuous. Even more important to the Inca were the highland system and the branches which connected it at many points to the coast road. At its maximum it ran from what is now the northern frontier of Ecuador, down through Quito, Cajamarca, Cuzco and other towns to Lake Titicaca, where it forked; one branch went north-east of the lake, through the Bolivian highlands to north-west Argentina, and the other went on the opposite side of the lake and eventually down the Chilean coast. Spurs connected the main road with the more important towns. The construction of mountain roads was a much more formidable problem than was presented by the coast roads, since they traversed very broken and difficult country. No great width was necessary, since the traffic consisted only of men and llamas, and in some places they were only about a yard wide, though the main route was doutless more than this. They had to zigzag up mountains and sometimes became stairways; they tunnelled through spurs or behind cliffs; they were enclosed between walls on the high plains, and were carried over swamps on stone-paved turf causeways, pierced by culverts for drainage.

Streams and valleys had to be crossed by bridges, and when they were narrow, these were stone slabs, some of which survived in Cuzco until a few years ago, or simple wooden constructions consisting of a pair of beams supporting cross-pieces. The wider valleys were crossed by suspension bridges, of which there was a famous example over the gorge of the River Apurimac, north-west of Cuzco, which was a formid-able obstacle to the Inca expansion until it was crossed in this way. Such bridges consisted of five great cables of vegetable fibre, sometimes obtained from an aloe called maguey, three supporting the floor and two serving as rails. They passed over four stone towers, two at each end, on a foundation platform, in which were embedded beams to which they were attached. The bridge was maintained by people who lived nearby, so paying their labour tax, and they had to renew the cables every year or two, a great undertaking with bridges which might be as much as 200 feet long. They swayed disconcertingly in the wind, and to cross them was a disagreeable experience; never-theless, the Spaniards could devise nothing better, and the Apurimac bridge was maintained until the latter part of the nineteenth century.

Rest houses, called tampo (Hispanicized into tambo), some-times accompanied by government storehouses, were built at intervals of four to eight miles along the roads for the use of official travellers—no others were allowed—and posts for the relay runners already mentioned were placed at intervals of a mile and a half, perhaps less. The posts consisted of a hut on either side of the road, each to house a pair of runners, called chasqui, who are said to have been capable of carrying a message 150 miles a day. When the Emperor, his family, and some few of the nobles travelled, they were carried in a canopied litter by four bearers, who were specialists at the task and worked in relays, but this was a privilege reserved for the highest in the land.

Several other features of Inca policy helped to weld the Empire into a coherent whole, although the process was not

I

complete when it was brought to an end. A well-known procedure, not unknown in the Old World, was to move potentially unruly sections of the population from a newly-conquered area into a settled one, replacing them by loyal colonists. People so moved were called mitimaes. It was suggested in a previous chapter that this may have been done in the Expansionist Period, but even if this were not so, it is one of the features which the Inca may well have learnt from the Chimú. The wisdom of the Inca is shown by the fact that they realized the effect of altitude on health, and mostly sent the mitimaes to a place on the same level as their home-land. Another factor which helped the coherence of the Empire was the spread of the Quechua language. To what extent this was deliberate policy is uncertain, but the Inca administrators spoke it, and it doubtless spread down through the minor officials to the commoners, partly from necessity and partly as a matter of prestige. The process was far from complete when the Spaniards arrived, and it was greatly extended by the Christian missionaries.

When conquered chiefs were retained in office as curacas, some of their sons were taken away to be educated like the nobles at Cuzco. Objects of worship belonging to conquered tribes were in some cases carried there also, with their attendant priests. In this way they both served as hostages and gave the provinces a feeling of community with Cuzco.

It is not possible to understand the nature of the Inca Empire without having some idea of the religion on which its whole life was based, and of which the ruler was an integral part. At the head of the supernatural hierarchy was a creator god, who had made not only earthly things but the other gods. He had various titles, but is generally known by the Hispanicized version of one of them, Viracocha, meaning Lord. He was rather remote from everyday things, and although he was represented by idols in human form in some of the temples, more attention was paid to the inferior gods, all in a sense his deputies. Pachacámac, the god of the great coastal sanctuary of the same name, had a great importance in the coast, and when the Inca absorbed him into their religious system, they fostered the impression that he was the same creator god, without ever calling him Viracocha. Below Viracocha came heavenly bodies, the sun, the moon, some of the stars and Venus, also the earth and the sea. The sun had a particular importance to the highlanders, partly because of its necessity for ripening the grain and of the chill which descends on the rarefied atmos, phere of the Andes when it is obscured, and partly because it was the personal god and ancestor of the Emperor and his family.

In spite of this, the famous temple at Cuzco, of which the remains are still to be seen in the Dominican friary there, was not primarily a sun temple, as it is generally called, since Vira, cocha held the chief place and the sun shared the remainder with the moon, the thunder, the stars and others. Judging by the existing remains, the buildings consisted of a number of rectangular rooms set round a court within an enclosure wall, and although it was built of the finest masonry and adorned with gold plates, the plan was that of the normal house com, pound, and it has rightly been described as a house of the gods made in the likeness of the houses of men. Such temples were truly the houses of the gods and their attendants, since their golden images were kept there, and were taken outside into the squares of the cities for the great public ceremonies.

Below the chief gods were a large number of local shrines and objects of veneration, called huacas from a Quechua word meaning shrine, although the varied objects to which it is applied are perhaps better described as holy things. They were extremely diverse in character, and included springs, rocks, hills, caves, tombs and the mummies of the dead. The mum, mies of previous Emperors had special honour. They were cared for, each by the royal ayllu composed of his descendants, and the later ones were kept in the palaces they had used during life, and treated as far as possible as if they were still alive. They were brought out into the squares of Cuzco to take part in the great festivals, like the images of the greater gods. There is a striking example of a holy rock at Kenko, near Cuzco, where a massive pointed limestone outcrop, twenty feet high, has its base encased in a rectangular masonry platform, and forms the focal point of an elliptical amphitheatre, which is enclosed by a low wall of Inca masonry. Mountain passes and difficult points on roads were and still are venerated by praying and adding a stone or a quid of coca to a pile of stones by the road, side, called apacita. There was also a wide variety of portable amulets, like the stone figures of alpacas already mentioned, and they included images of maize cobs or potatoes, crystals, and curiously shaped natural stones.

Temples and shrines were cared for by priests of various grades, at the head of whom was a high priest who was gener, ally a near relative of the Emperor, and their duties included divination, sacrifice and curing, as well as the care of the shrines. The public expression of religion consisted of festivals, of which there was one associated with each of the twelve months, in addition to special ones held in times of emergency, such as drought or pestilence. The months were lunar, but twelve lunar months are about eleven days short of a solar year and it is not known how the two were reconciled. Preparation for a festival included fasting from certain foods and sexual intercourse, and the ceremonies themselves chiefly took the form of processions, sacrifices and dances. Llamas were the most common sacrificial victims, but guinea, pigs and commo, dities such as maize beer, called chicha, were also sacrificed. Human sacrifice was practised, but only in serious crises and on very special occasions, the victims being either children or those who had been reserved from among the Chosen Women.

Plate 68

Plate 63

There can be little doubt that this provides the explanation of a find made by Uhle when he was excavating the Inca cemetery at Pachacámac, namely, the mummies of a number of richly-dressed young women, who had been strangled and yet buried with every appearance of honour. It is known that they had a convent which helped to serve the 'Sun Temple' at this important site.

Apart from the public ceremonies of religion, private practices included purification and divination. Sin against their moral code was regarded as provoking the anger of the gods, disqualifying the offender from taking part in ceremonies, and perhaps causing bodily harm to himself and illness to the Emperor. It was purged by confession of sins of word and deed to a priest, followed by penance and washing in running water. Divination took many forms, ranging from the solemn consultation by the Emperor of one of the great official oracles in his temple before undertaking a campaign, to the counting of a pile of maize kernels by a humble villager to determine, according to whether the number was odd or even, if the day was propitious for him to begin his planting or not.

The motives which impelled the Incas to undertake their great conquests and the reasons for their success now require consideration. They used much the same weapons and tactics as their opponents, so the reason cannot be sought in superior armaments. Slings and the bolas were used for distant fighting, and they adopted the use of the spear-thrower from their coastal subjects. They did not themselves use the bow, but they had some soldiers from the margins of the eastern forests who did. At close quarters they used star-headed maces of stone or copper on wooden handles, sword-clubs of hardwood, stone or copper battle-axes of various forms, and lances. They protected themselves with quilted cotton armour, helmets of quilted cotton or plaited cane, and small round or square wooden shields covered with skin or cloth.

Plate 70

Plate 1, 71

Towns and villages were not fortified, and defensive works consisted of hill-top forts, called in Quechua pucara, to which the inhabitants fled when attacked. These forts are exemplified, on the grandest scale, by Saccsaihuaman, with its three great ramparts on one side and a precipice on the other, crowning the hill above Cuzco, which was built in its present form by Pachacuti more for show than from necessity. The city of Machu Picchu, down the Urubamba Valley near the frontiers of the highland dominion, may appear to be an exception by reason of its very strong and inaccessible position on a saddle bordered by two precipices, but this is a consequence of the topography and it has no defensive walls.

Once the Inca conquests had begun, the fundamental factor in their continued success was their sustained offensive spirit, which contrasted with the raiding pattern general in highland warfare. This was combined with superior transport and supply facilities, afforded by their roads and stores of food, so that they were able to place an overwhelming force in a given place when they wished. Apart from the Emperor's picked bodyguard of nobles, there was no standing army, but there was an organization which ensured that sufficient trained men were available when required. All able-bodied men were trained to arms, and the main body of any force consisted of mit'a levies, organized according to the provinces they came from in squadrons, which were subdivided in the same decimal system as the population at large, under officers of similar grades. These levies were marched about under strict discipline, but the actual mode of fighting was similar to that of other Andean tribes; it started at a distance with showers of sling stones, bolas and darts, and when the opponents came to close quarters each man fought individually. One successful tactical modification introduced by the Incas was to divide their forces, one part engaging the enemy while the other was held in reserve and thrown in at a critical moment.

The motives for the sustained aggressiveness of the Inca are another question. The first conquests of neighbouring tribes could have been undertaken from motives of vengeance and a desire to consolidate their position, but the personality of Pachacuti must also be taken into account. As power and wealth increased, there seems to have developed a thirst for more, and each new conquest enriched the State and added to the glory of the Emperor. The royal ayllus and the Incas by privilege grew up into an hereditary aristocracy, exempt from the labour tax, and being polygamous, they increased rapidly. They were educated in the arts of war, and the fighting spirit was encouraged. Wars not only employed and restrained seditious tendencies, which are known to have existed, but provided posts of responsibility in the administration of the conquered provinces. The structure of the ruling classes was thus in an unbalanced condition, which required expansion in order to maintain stability, and developments designed to rectify this might well have taken place if the Empire had lasted longer.

The Empire was, indeed, still in course of evolution, when the end came. It had two great weaknesses. One was that there was no fixed method by which the Emperor designated his successor, and any of his sons by his chief wife could be chosen. When Huayna Capac died suddenly without naming his successor, this led to the strife between Huascar and Atahuallpa each supported by a powerful faction, which left the Empire in a weakened state when the Spaniards arrived. It was unlucky for the Inca that they came at that time, since Atahuallpa would doubtless have been universally recognized within a few years. The other weakness was excessive centralization in the Emperor. Every official was responsible to the one above him and so up to the Emperor, but there was little or no cohesion between those of the same grade. It was a pyramid, but it was built of disconnected rods, and when struck at the apex it fell to pieces. Before the coming of the Spaniards this mattered little; it was unthinkable that any outside enemy should lay hands on the divine Emperor, but the Europeans saw him as a misguided heathen and they had no scruples. After the fall of Atahuallpa in 1532, resistance was maintained in isolated places for forty years more. Pizarro set up Manco, a grandson of Huayna Capac, as a puppet ruler, but he rebelled and gathered a considerable following, laying siege to Cuzco and Lima. This rising was a serious threat to the Spaniards, but it was dispersed, and Manco fled down the Urubamba Valley, eventually taking refuge at an inaccessible place called Vitcos, where he, and after his death his sons, maintained a precarious rule until 1572. After his flight, the issue was never in doubt. The Spaniards gained rapidly in strength and the old civilizations of the Central Andes had gone for ever.

AFTER THE CONQUEST

See *Bibliography, Handbook of South American Indians*

While resistance was maintained by the few in the Urubamba Valley, the bulk of the population fell under the Spanish yoke, and Rowe has aptly said that the Indians exchanged a despotism of predictable demands and justice for another of limitless demands and justice reserved to their oppressors. In the first years of the colony, roads were neglected, much irrigated land fell into disuse, and the population of the occupied provinces was drastically reduced. Recent studies indicate that the reduction was mainly due to the flight of Indians to the remoter districts, especially to the lowlands east of the Andes, but forced labour, in the shape of the old mit'a intensified, particularly in the mines and at unaccustomed altitudes, doubtless took its toll in deaths. Much information about conditions at this time, the life of the Indians under the Incas and afterwards, their customs, and the good and bad sides of

Spanish rule, is given by the numerous line-drawings in a work by Felipe Guaman Poma de Ayala, dating from the end of the sixteenth century. See *Bibliography*, Guaman Poma de Ayala, 1936

Apart from mass baptisms without instruction, which had little effect, the conversion of the Indians to Christianity was slow at first, and it was not until late in the sixteenth century that much progress was made. Even then, a great many of the old beliefs survived, the worship of the heavenly bodies and the huacas continued, and it was not until about the middle of the seventeenth century, after an intensive campaign for 'the extirpation of idolatry', that true Christian doctrines were generally understood and held. Some of the old practices, including fertility ceremonies, continued after this time—in fact they still do—but they had degenerated into mere superstitions, and were tolerated because they were no longer regarded as 'idolatry'. The state of affairs in the intermediate period is illustrated by the case of a huddled mummy bundle found on the coast, which bore the appearance of a normal late pre-Conquest burial. When it was unwrapped, a printed indulgence bearing the date 1580 was found next to the body.

Material features of the old culture also survived in places. The art of weaving remained at a high level, and fine ponchos and other textiles, bearing a combination of European and indigenous features, have survived in some numbers. The wooden kero, or waisted beaker, continued to be made, and there are many fine examples, with elaborate designs inlaid in polychrome lacquer, whose post-Conquest origin is shown by representations of stringed musical instruments and European dress. Pottery also was made in hybrid forms, particularly in the area of the old Chimú state. There are examples of black ware jars with a bearded Spanish face on the neck, and there are double whistling jars of characteristically Chimú-Inca forms, made, not in the customary black ware, but in a buff-coloured ware covered with a European green glaze.

Most of the Indians at first continued to live on their village lands under their curacas, but as time went on an increasing number left the land and became servants in Spanish households. This class, called yananconas, earned certain advantages including exemption from the mit'a, and they tended to increase and to become a landless urban proletariat, until eventually, late in the sixteenth century, their numbers had to be checked by legislation.

By no means all of the old Inca nobility were killed or followed Manco to his refuge at Vitcos, and many of them came to terms with the conquerors, some of whom took wives from among them. The Inca Garcilaso de la Vega, well known for his writings about the Incas, was the son of such a union, and he spent most of his days in Spain. The Incas, the curacas and the yananconas, all tended towards integration with Spanish society, and those of higher degree appeared on occasion in Spanish dress. Many of the curacas, indeed, proved themselves worse oppressors of their brethren than their Spanish overlords; for example, one of them was deposed for 'extorsions, violence, and tyrannies . . . to the point of committing the cruel act of branding them on the buttocks like mules'.

Descendants of the Inca nobility were still recognized in the eighteenth century, when some of them held important offices and lived in considerable state. There seems to have been a kind of romantic revival of interest in the past, since portraits of the period depict them richly dressed in Inca style, with some European details, with their Spanish coats of arms beside them. When increasing oppression provoked rebellions of the Indians in the eighteenth century, nobles of this sort provided the leadership. It is worthy of note that most of these risings, including the final great revolt of 1780 under José Gabriel Tupac Amaru, were directed against the local administration while remaining loyal to Church and Crown, both of which were regarded as in some degree the protectors of the Indians at that time. The

Inca nobles have long since disappeared, and now under the Republic the distinction between the Indians and those of mixed blood, the mestizos, is somewhat blurred, but there are still many distinctively Indian communities, which reflect the tradition of the ancient ayllus, the base of the pyramid of Inca society.

Bibliography

BENNETT, WENDELL, C., "Excavations at Wari, Ayacucho", *Yale University Publications in Anthropology*, No. 49, 1953.
Ancient Arts of the Andes, Museum of Modern Art, New York, 1954.
"A Reappraisal of Peruvian Archaeology," (Editor), *American Antiquity*, Vol. XIII, No. 4, Part 2. April, 1948.

BENNETT, WENDELL C. AND J. B. BIRD, *Andean Culture History*, American Museum of Natural History, Handbook Series, No. 15, New York, 1949.

BIRD, J. AND L. BELLINGER, *Paracas Fabrics and Nazca Needlework*, The Textile Museum, Washington, D.C., 1954.

BUSHNELL, G. H. S. AND A. DIGBY, *Ancient American Pottery*,* Faber and Faber, London, 1955.

COLLIER, DONALD, "Cultural Chronology and Change as reflected in the Ceramics of the Virú Valley, Peru," *Fieldiana: Anthropology*, Vol. XLIII. Chicago Natural History Museum, 1955.

DOERING, H. U., *The Art of Ancient Peru*,* Zwemmer, London, 1952.

GUAMAN, POMA DE AYALA, FELIPE, "Nueva corónica y buen gobierno," *Institut d'Ethnologie Fravaux Mémoires,* Vol. XXIII. Paris, 1936.

HANDBOOK OF SOUTH AMERICAN INDIANS, Volume 2, Smithsonian Institution, Bureau of American Ethnology, Bulletin, 143. Especially articles by Bennett, Larco Hoyle, Kubler, Rowe and Valcárcel.

JOHNSON, FREDERICK, "Radiocarbon Dating," (Editor), *American Antiquity*, Vol. XVII, No. 1, Part 2, July, 1951. (Article by J. Bird on S. America.)

Bibliography

KUBLER, G., *Cuzco*, UNESCO Museums and Monuments—III, H.M. Stationery Office.

LEHMANN, W. AND H. U. DOERING, *The Art of Old Peru*,* Benn, London, 1924.

REICHLEN, H. AND P., "Recherches Archéologiques dans les Andes de Cajamarca," *Journal de la Société des Américanistes*, Nouvelle Série t. XXXVIII, 1949, p. 137, Paris.

STRONG, W. D. AND C. EVANS, JR., *Cultural Stratigraphy in the Virú Valley*, Columbia University, New York, 1952.

WILLEY, GORDON R., *Prehistoric Settlements in the Virú Valley*, Smithsonian Institution, Bureau of American Ethnology, Bulletin 155, 1953.

In this list, *Andean Culture History*, the *Handbook of South American Indians*, and *Prehistoric Settlement Patterns in the Virú Valley* contain especially full bibliographies. References given in them are not repeated here unless there is strong reason for doing so. Publications which are virtually unobtainable are omitted. Those marked with an asterisk are included because they contain useful illustrations.

SOURCES OF ILLUSTRATIONS

Original photographs for the plates were supplied by the Author, 69; Rafael Larco Hoyle, 4–8, 11–15, 17, 29; American Geographical Society, 51; Cambridge University Museum of Archaeology and Ethnology, 19, 21–5, 30–2, 37–8, 40–1, 43–4, 46–9, 54–5, 57–61, 63, 65–7; A. Costa, 36; John R. Freeman, 33–4, 45, 50, 64; Hans Mann, 1–3, 9, 10, 18, 35, 52–3, 56, 62, 71; Musée de l'Homme, 26–8, 39, 42; Peabody Museum, Harvard University, 20; Philadelphia University Museum, 16; Nicholas Young, 68, 70.

Figures 1, 3, 5–9, 12, 13 were drawn by Mrs. G. E. Daniel, Fig. 11 is reproduced by courtesy of the Medici Society and was originally published in T. Joyce, 'South American Archaeology'.

THE PLATES

4

7

9

10

13

14

15

16

19

20

22

23

24

25

26

27

28

29

30

31

32

33

34

35

36

37

38

39

40

41

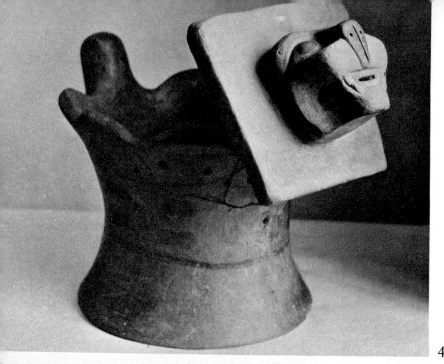

42

43

45

46

47

48

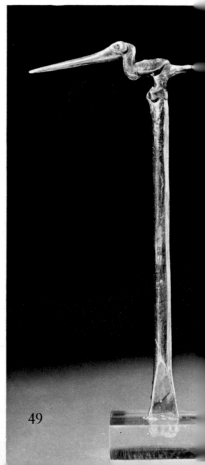

49

51

52

54

55

56

58

59

60

61

63

64

65

66

67

68

69

NOTES ON THE PLATES

Notes on the Plates

Note

Where dimensions are not given, they are not available, but it can be assumed that pots of the same or similar type, e.g. stirrup spouts, are of comparable size throughout the succession.   C.M.A.E.—Cambridge University Museum of Archaeology and Ethnology.

1   View from the late Inca city of Machu Picchu up the Urubamba Gorge. Inca masonry of the finest type, forming part of a shrine, on the right.

2   The high plateau (*puna*) in the Titicaca region, showing llamas.

3   Quebrada de Pescadores, Southern Peru. Small valley, showing the marked contrast between the irrigated valley bottom and the surrounding barren hills.

4   Stirrup-spouted jar representing woman suckling child. Cupisnique Culture, Chicama Valley. Rafael Larco Hoyle Collection.

5   Bottle, showing highly stylized incised designs, probably feline eyes and claws, surrounded by rocker stamping. Cupisnique Culture, Chicama Valley. Rafael Larco Hoyle Collection.

6   Vase representing aged woman's face. Cupisnique Culture, Chicama Valley. Rafael Larco Hoyle Collection.

7   Stirrup-spouted jar with applied knobs and highly roughened surface. Cupisnique Culture, Chicama Valley. Rafael Larco Hoyle Collection.

8   Stirrup-spouted jar with incised designs, probably feline motifs. Cupisnique Culture. Chicama Valley. Rafael Larco Hoyle Collection.

9   Row of engraved stones. Temple at Cerro Sechín, Casma Valley. Coastal Chavín Culture.

10 Engraved stones representing man cut in half, and trophy head. Temple at Cerro Sechín, Casma Valley. Coastal Chavín Culture.

11 Stirrup-spouted jar with engraved and partly painted concentric circles. Salinar Culture. Rafael Larco Hoyle Collection.

12 Stirrup-spouted jar representing a monkey standing on a circular vessel, which is actually annular since it is formed around a central opening. Salinar Culture, Chicama Valley. Rafael Larco Hoyle Collection.

13 Spout and bridge jar representing a monkey. Gallinazo or Virú Culture. Rafael Larco Hoyle Collection.

14 Spout and bridge jar, representing feline. Gallinazo or Virú Culture. Rafael Larco Hoyle Collection.

15 Double spout and bridge jar, with engraved design. Paracas Cavernas. Rafael Larco Hoyle Collection.

16 Polychrome bowl decorated with resinous colours outlined by incisions, applied after firing. The designs represent snake heads. Paracas Cavernas. Height 4½ in. University Museum, Philadelphia.

17 Spout and bridge jar decorated negatively in black on a red ground. Represents a warrior riding on a small reed *balsa* raft (*caballito*). Gallinazo or Virú Culture. Rafael Larco Hoyle Collection.

18 Boy on *balsa* raft (*caballito*). Peruvian Coast.

19 Embroidered polychrome textile borders, in rose red, dark blue, green, yellow-brown and other colours. The upper one shows a pair of interlacing snakes enclosing naturalistic animals, and the lower one feline monsters. Width of upper piece, 5½ in. Paracas Necropolis. C.M.A.E.

20 Double spout and bridge jar, painted white with the tips of the spouts red. Diameter, 8 in. Paracas Necropolis. Peabody Museum, Harvard University.

21 Rare figurine of pinkish-white pottery with details picked out in red and buff, and outlined by incised lines. Height, 3½ in. Paracas Cavernas. C.M.A.E.

22 Red and white jar, representing feline god holding copper hand axe and severed human head. Height, 15½ in. Mochica Culture. C.M.A.E.

23 Red and white jar, stirrup spout broken, representing naturalistic jaguar attacking man. A rare type. Height of jaguar, 8 in. Mochica Culture. C.M.A.E.

24 Red and white stirrup-spouted jar, depicting warrior holding club, standing on globular vessel decorated with stylized rays in low relief. Height, 11½ in. Mochica Culture. C.M.A.E.

25 Red and white stirrup-spouted jar, decorated in relief with demon catching fish. Height, 9 in. Mochica Culture. C.M.A.E.

26-8 Modelled vessels with negative decoration in black over white and red. Recuay Culture.

29 Interior of bowl painted in brown on white in cursive style. Rafael Larco Hoyle Collection.

30 Double spout and bridge jar, painted with humming birds in two shades of red, black, white, yellow, purple and grey. Height, 5 in. Nazca Culture. C.M.A.E.

31 'One man band', a spout and bridge polychrome jar. Height, 6½ in. Late Nazca (Nazca Y) Culture. C.M.A.E.

32 Double spout and bridge jar, representing a trophy head, the lips fixed together with wooden pins or thorns. Height, 5 in. Nazca Culture. C.M.A.E.

33 Cap made of pile cloth. Probably Coast Tiahuanaco Period. Height, 3½ in. British Museum.

34 Shell inlaid with a face and surrounding mosaic of multi-coloured shell fragments. Width 4½ in. Nazca Culture. British Museum.

35 Geometrical markings as seen from the air. Nazca Valley.

36 The monolithic gateway of Tiahuanaco, with wall footings and other carved stones.

37 Sherd painted in black and red, outlined by incision, on a reddish buff ground. The feline face is about 2 in. wide. Pucara. C.M.A.E.

38 Spittoon-shaped vessel, painted in black, white, red and orange, on a reddish buff ground. Height, 4½ in. Early Tiahuanaco. C.M.A.E.

39 Polychrome bowl decorated with a puma and geometrical designs. Classic Tiahuanaco.

40 Work basket, containing spools wound with spun thread and other weaving materials. Length, 14 in. C.M.A.E.

41 Piece of tapestry in at least two shades of yellow or brown, with black, white and rose pink. Coast Tiahuanaco. C.M.A.E.

42 Puma-headed polychrome bowl. Classic Tiahuanaco.

43 Head-vase painted in black, white and red. Height, 5½ in. Coast Tiahuanaco B, or Epigonal. From Huacho, Central Coast. C.M.A.E.

44 Bottle, decorated with designs in pressed relief and painted with sub-dued colours, black, white, orange and grey, over a red slip. Height, 7½ in. North Coast Tiahuanaco B. (Variant of the more usual black, white, red over buff). C.M.A.E.

45 Silver beaker of type common in post-Classic times in many parts of the Coast. Height, 8 in.
Gold wrist ornament. Nazca. Both, British Museum.

46 Gold mask for sewing to a garment. Height, 7 in. From Ica, South Coast. Probably City Builder Period. C.M.A.E.

47 Copper staff head, bearing macaws, parrots and other birds. Height, 6 in. Chimú. C.M.A.E.

48 Gold male figurine and silver female one. Height, $2\frac{1}{2}$ in. Inca. C.M.A.E.

49 Gold lime spoon. The lime was chewed with coca leaves. Height, 3 in. C.M.A.E.

50 Wooden centre-board and two steering sweeps for raft. Height of centre-board, 52 in. Probably from Ica. British Museum.

51 Air view of part of Chan Chan, the Chimú capital.

52 Wall with mud-plaster reliefs. Chimú Period. Chan Chan.

53 Detail of mud-plaster relief. Chan Chan.

54 Black-white-red jar. Height, 12 in. Late Coast Tiahuanaco (B) style. Central Coast. C.M.A.E.

55 Stirrup-spouted blackware jar with pressed relief design. Height, $9\frac{1}{2}$ in. Chimú. C.M.A.E.

56 Air view of Chimú frontier fortress of Paramonga.

57 Feather shirt *(poncho)* and head-dress, decorated with stylized owls. Chimú. C.M.A.E.

58 Llama-head blackware bowl. Height, $5\frac{1}{2}$ in. Chimú. C.M.A.E.

59 Black-on-white bowl. Height, $6\frac{1}{2}$ in. City Builder Period. From Chancay Valley, Central Coast. C.M.A.E.

60 Polychrome bowl. Height, 3½ in. Ica style, City Builder Period, South Coast. C.M.A.E.

61 Polychrome bowl painted with blurred textile designs. Height, 3½ in. Ica style, City Builder Period, South Coast. C.M.A.E.

62 Ruined circular burial chamber (*chullpa*). Lake Titicaca region.

63 Alpaca made of banded agate. Length, 5½ in. Inca. C.M.A.E.

64 Stone dish with figure designs including llama and woman spinning. Inca. Diameter, 20 in. British Museum.

65 Cuzco Polychrome saucer. Diameter, 3½ in. Inca. C.M.A.E.

66 Cuzco Polychrome bottle. Height, 4 in. Inca. C.M.A.E.

67 Cuzco Polychrome aryballus. Height, 14 in. Inca. C.M.A.E.

68 Sacred rock at Kenko, near Cuzco. Inca.

69 Street scene, Cuzco, showing late Inca masonry of finest type. Reputed palace of Huayna Capac on left, and substructure of convent of Santa Catalina, formerly the Accla Huasi or house of the Chosen Women, on right.

70 Late Inca masonry facing of lowest rampart of fortress of Saccsaihuaman, dominating Cuzco.

71 Late Inca city of Machu Picchu.

Index